North American Droughts

AAAS Selected Symposia Series

Published by Westview Press
5500 Central Avenue, Boulder, Colorado

for the

American Association for the Advancement of Science
1776 Massachusetts Ave., N.W., Washington, D.C.

North American Droughts

Edited by Norman J. Rosenberg

AAAS Selected Symposium **15**

AAAS Selected Symposia Series

Published in 1978 in the United States of America by

Westview Press, Inc.
5500 Central Avenue
Boulder, Colorado 80301
Frederick A. Praeger, Publisher and Editorial Director

Library of Congress Catalog Card Number: 78-52024
ISBN: 0-89158-443-9

Printed and bound in the United States of America

About the Book

Recognizing drought as a characteristic feature of the North American climate, the contributors to this volume seek to organize available evidence of both prehistoric and modern drought events and to provide information on the severity of droughts, especially those which have occurred since weather records have been kept. The impacts of modern-era droughts on production and the potential impact of future droughts on the productivity of North American agriculture are examined.

The authors explore the effects of past droughts on the social, cultural, and political life of the population; the possible effects of drought on today's energy- and technology-intensive society; and the ramifications of drought for the national economy. The social and political strategies that local, state, and federal governments may use to ameliorate the effects of drought are also considered, as are some possible technological defenses against drought--weather modification, expanded irrigation, new techniques of water harvesting and storage, and new agronomic adaptations. Finally, the critical question of whether future droughts can be forecast is examined.

Contents

List of Figures

Chapter 8

List of Tables

Foreword

The *AAAS Selected Symposia Series* was begun in 1977 to
provide a means for more permanently recording and more
widely disseminating some of the valuable material which is
discussed at the AAAS Annual National Meetings. The volumes
in this *Series* are based on symposia held at the Meetings
which address topics of current and continuing significance,
both within and among the sciences, and in the areas in which
science and technology impact on public policy. The *Series*
format is designed to provide for rapid dissemination of information, so the papers are not typeset but are reproduced
directly from the camera copy submitted by the authors, without copy editing. The papers are reviewed and edited by
the symposia organizers who then become the editors of the
various volumes. Most papers published in this *Series* are
original contributions which have not been previously published, although in some cases additional papers from other
sources have been added by an editor to provide a more comprehensive view of a particular topic. Symposia may be reports of new research or reviews of established work, particularly work of an interdisciplinary nature, since the AAAS
Annual Meeting typically embraces the full range of the
sciences and their societal implications.

WILLIAM D. CAREY
Executive Officer
American Association for
the Advancement of Science

About the Editor and Authors

Norman J. Rosenberg is a professor of agricultural meteorology at the Institute of Agriculture and Natural Resources, University of Nebraska, Lincoln. He specializes in micrometeorology and microclimate modification to improve water use efficiency and is currently developing strategies to combat the effects of drought on agriculture in the Western United States. He works with the U.S. Agency for International Development, the National Oceanic and Atmospheric Administration, and the National Academy of Sciences/National Research Council as a consultant on drought mitigation projects for developing countries. He has published some 80 papers on windbreaks, evapotranspiration, and photosynthesis, and is the author of Microclimate: The Biological Environment (Wiley-Interscience, 1974).

L. Dean Bark, professor of physics and climatologist with the Kansas Agricultural Experiment Station at Kansas State University, has conducted research in agricultural and statistical climatology, and the climate and economic effects of weather modification in Kansas. He is a member of several committees which are concerned with these problems.

A. Berry Crawford is director of the Institute for Policy Research, Western Governors Policy Office, Denver, while on leave from Utah State University, where he is a professor. He is responsible for preparation of the Directory of Federal Drought Assistance and is chairman of an advisory panel to the Water Resources Research Task Force of the White House. He is the author of over 50 publications on western public policy issues, including Values and Choices in the Development of an Arid Land River Basin (D.F. Peterson, coeditor; University of Arizona Press, in press).

Richard E. Felch, agricultural weather liaison officer with the Statistical Reporting Service, U.S. Department of

*Agriculture, has studied drought and drought related problems
since 1972. He is a former editor of the* Weekly Weather and
Crop Bulletin, *and will soon be joining the World Food and
Agricultural Outlook and Situation Board, USDA.*

*J. Eugene Haas, senior scientist at the Natural Hazards
Research Institute, is also professor of sociology and head
of the Research Program on Technology, Environment and Man,
Institute of Behavioral Science, at the University of Colorado. His work has focused on socioeconomic aspects of natural
hazards and disasters and he has researched disasters worldwide. His most recent book is* Reconstruction Following
Disaster *(with R.W. Kates and M.J. Bowden; MIT Press, 1977).*

*Robert D. Miewald is associate professor of political
science at the University of Nebraska, Lincoln. He specializes in public administration, and natural resources management, and is the author of* Public Administration: A Critical
Perspective *(McGraw-Hill, 1978).*

*James E. Newman, professor of agronomy and climatology
at Purdue University, is the author of some 100 articles on
bioclimatology and agronomic-related problems. He is chairman of the study panel on the impact of climatic fluctuation
on major North American food crops at the Institute of Ecology, and has been editor-in-chief of* Agricultural Meteorology.
*He is a fellow of the American Society of Agronomy and received their Soils and Crops national award for excellence
in scientific journalism.*

*Roger F. Riefler is a professor in the Department of
Economics at the University of Nebraska, Lincoln. His specific area of specialization is urban and regional economics,
and he has recently published "Interregional Input-Output:
A State of the Arts Survey," in G.G. Judge and T. Takayama
(Eds.),* Studies in Economic Planning Over Space and Time
(North Holland, 1973).

*Stephen H. Schneider, deputy head of the Climate Project
at the National Center for Atmospheric Research in Boulder,
has had extensive involvement in the field of climatology.
He is a consultant on climatic change, food shortages, and
potential climate-related interstate conflicts, a member of
the Carter-Mondale Task Force on Science Policy, and the
editor of* Climatic Change, *an international journal. He is
the author of some 50 papers and of* The Genesis Strategy:
Climate and Global Survival *(with L.E. Mesirow; Plenum, 1976).*

Dust storm, Cimarron County, Oklahoma, 1936 [Arthur Rothstein; courtesy of Library of Congress]

Introduction

Norman J. Rosenberg

This volume is primarily a compilation of papers presented at a symposium entitled - American Droughts - which
took place in Denver on the morning of February 21, 1977 as
one of the first sessions of the 1977 annual meeting of the
American Association for the Advancement of Science. The
symposium generated considerable excitement. We who partici-
pated would have liked to believe that our collective repu-
tation as scientists and scholars was responsible for
attracting an overflow audience as well as large numbers of
journalists and television people representing the national
press and the networks. We must admit, however, that it was
drought which provided the stimulus for this attention.

By mid-February of 1977 the midwestern United States
was experiencing one of the most severe droughts in its
recorded history. Many aspects of the drought were reminis-
cent of the Great Plains drought of the 1930's. During the
week of the AAAS meeting, for example, dramatic dust storms
blew up in eastern Colorado and western Kansas and Oklahoma
and moved eastward across the country. Some were large
enough to be seen in satellite images. The midwestern
drought was actually most severe in Minnesota and the Dakotas
but was felt with growing urgency in parts of Nebraska,
Kansas, eastern Colorado and Wyoming and as far east as
Illinois. At the time of our symposium the seriousness of
drought in the western and intermountain states was also
gaining national attention. The plight of the Rocky mountain
ski-resorts, lacking snow, drew national attention. So, too,
did the reports of water rationing in certain California
communities.
    The unprecedented extent of drought affecting, as it
did, most of the nation west of the Mississippi and parts to
the east, led to general national concern about drought of
a sort which had not been experienced in many years. In

1

Denver on February 20 (the day prior to our symposium, but by no design of the symposium convener) the Governors of the western states met in an emergency session to discuss the drought situation. The Governors called for emergency actions to be taken by the States and by the Federal government to provide relief and assistance to drought-impacted farmers and to cities whose water supplies were threatened. The new Administration in Washington, only one month in office, was challenged by the Governors to address the now serious national problem of drought.

Most of what was said by the speakers at our crowded and sometimes hectic symposium on American Drought was true and much of it was wise. None of the speakers could have anticipated, however, that between the time of the symposium and the publication of its proceedings so many events would occur which would serve to support their assumptions or to challenge them. By the fall of 1977 the general drought picture in the United States had changed significantly.

Generally good rains occurred in the Great Plains region during the spring and summer of 1977. The winter wheat crop of the southern Great Plains, which had appeared in danger of failure in February, turned out, in fact, to be one of the best in history. The corn crop did well, in general, because of a good distribution of summer rains. Further, the rapid response of the new Administration and the Congress to the drought problem and the nature and scope of the programs initiated before, during and after the growing season of 1977 would have appeared unlikely in February. Because so much has happened since the symposium the editor has invited Dr. A. B. Crawford to describe the actual state and federal responses to the drought of 1977. Upon completion of the symposium it was decided that the economic perspective on drought had not been covered in sufficient detail. Hence, Dr. Roger Riefler's chapter has also been added to the Proceedings.

It is probably a general failing of symposia that papers delivered tend to overlap or, perhaps, to be occasionally repetitive. The sensitive reader may object, for example, that fully half of the contributors to this volume complain that "drought is a non-event" and bemoan the fact that, because of this peculiar characteristic of drought, it is difficult to know when to take action and what action to take. Such an overlapping of views or of subjects for review, on the other hand, provides some benefit since it measures the range of agreement or disagreement between disciplinarians attempting to grapple with a very complex problem.

The title of the volume has been changed from the original American Droughts to North American Droughts. We are
saved from the charge of false advertising by Professor
Newman's inclusion in Chapter 3 of the Canadian wheat crop
in his evaluation of drought related yield reductions in
North America. Dr. Schneider's Chapter 9 on the predictability of drought is applicable to the continent. In recent
months some of us who, despite the rains, continue our work
to develop drought preparedness plans, have become aware of
well organized activities of drought surveillance and relief
conducted under the auspices of the agency - Emergency
Planning Canada.

The problems of the Canadian Great Plains with respect
to drought are quite similar to those of the northern Great
Plains in the United States. Practices adopted to diminish
the impact of drought in the 1930's were instituted in
Canada as well and there exists a strong community of interest and effective exchange of information between agricultural researchers, at least, in the Canadian and American
Great Plains. Unhappily, this volume has not addressed the
occurrence of and reactions to drought in Mexico and Central
America.

Perhaps one further explanation is in order. It is not
a coincidence that three of the nine chapters of this volume
are written by Professors at the University of Nebraska-
Lincoln. Since the occurrence of a severe drought in Nebraska and adjoining states in 1974 we have been attempting at
the University to organize coordinated research projects to
provide the basic information needed for development of
'drought-strategies' which can be implemented on the state
level. Because of this effort a large number of scholars
have focused their disciplinary skills on analysis of the
various aspects of drought. Professors Miewald and Riefler
were among the large number who contributed to the Nebraska
effort. Their scholarly search of the literature and analyses have been helpful in the work of their colleagues in the
physical and social sciences.

The chapters which follow:

In Chapter 1 Professor L. Dean Bark of Kansas State
University has reviewed evidence of the occurrence of prehistoric droughts as well as droughts which have occurred in
historic times in North America. He has also given us some
interesting insights into the perceptions of drought by the
'boomers' and 'gloomers' who settled the Plains. Professor
Bark's chapter demonstrates that drought is a recurrent and,
we may assume, inevitable feature of the climate of the North

American mid-continent.

In Chapter 2 Dr. Richard Felch of the U.S. Department of Agriculture defines drought in quantitative terms. He has used the Palmer Drought Severity Index as a tool for mapping the temporal and aerial occurrence of drought across the continental United States. His comparison of the droughts of the 1930's, 1950's and mid 1970's show the latter, in certain places at least, to be as severe as any on record.

Professor James E. Newman of Purdue University has re-viewed, in Chapter 3, the impact of droughts on agricultural productivity in North America through analysis of the long term variability and trends in grain crop production. Since more than 90% of all grain in the world export trade origi-nates from North America the reliability of this production is of critical importance to world food supplies. Professor Newman has shown that the greatest seasonal or climatic fluc-tuation associated with negative deviations of corn yields is drought. Newman suggests further, on the basis of 11-year running average yield analyses, that good seasonal weather and bad seasonal weather years to not occur at random in time or space and that, historically, in North America they have occurred over series of years roughly in alternate decades. The fact that the good and bad years have not occurred historically across all of the North American grain producing areas in the same year has provided a fortunate degree of stability.

Professor Roger F. Riefler at the University of Nebras-ka-Lincoln examines, in Chapter 4, the economic implications of drought. The initial manifestation of drought creates a supply problem. However, the ultimate impact of the drought, especially at national and international levels, is deter-mined by the demand side of the ledger. Professor Riefler feels that, to be effective, any assessment of the economic impact of drought must look at the problems of both supply and demand. In his view, the economic tools are available with which to measure and analyze the impacts of drought and to prescribe techniques to minimize its most serious impacts on the economy.

In Chapter 5 Professor Robert D. Miewald of the Univer-sity of Nebraska-Lincoln considers that drought has the potential to cause profound upsets in our political, social and economic systems, whatever the attempts made to mitigate its effects. Miewald asks whether the resiliency evidenced by the nation in recovering from the effects of the 1930's drought continues to this day. In developing this thesis, Professor Miewald identifies a wide range of political and

social interactions   and responses to droughts which have
occurred in the United States in historic times. He evaluates responses to drought made by individuals and by communities and examines, as well, the impact of drought on inter-
community relations. Further, he considers the regional
effect of drought and the ways in which public officials have
been called upon traditionally to respond. Finally, Professor Miewald considers the possible impact of drought in
the 1970's and in the coming years upon United States international relations and foreign policy.

Professor J. Eugene Haas of the University of Colorado
summarizes,in Chapter 6,a wide range of strategies which may
be applicable in the event of drought. His paper draws upon
work done largely by the Institute of Behavioral Sciences of
the University of Colorado and published in a number of very
useful monographs referenced by Haas. The work reported in
this chapter places drought in perspective as one of some
fifteen types of disasters which can affect the nation.
This analysis considers many possible impacts of the various
disasters, e.g. property damage which might be expected per
capita, the range of social consequences and, ultimately,
the techniques for preparedness or avoidance of disaster.
Professor Haas lists possible responses to drought which
might be effected through modifications of the meteorological
and hydrological components of drought. Water augmentation
and water conservation are included in this category. He
also discusses possible modifications in agricultural operations and ways of spreading or sharing losses and costs.
Additionally, Professor Haas discusses the impact of drought
on urban areas and adaptations which may be considered.

Professor Haas' summary indicates the need for a wide
range of strategies to cope with drought at every level and
for a mixing of adjustments or strategies which ought to be
adopted prior to the onset of a drought period, if at all
possible. The development of long range climate forecasting
and the application of land use regulations should receive
the greatest emphasis, according to Haas, if our objective
is to reduce the catastrophic potential of drought and to
improve economic benefits.

Professor Norman J. Rosenberg of the University of
Nebraska-Lincoln describes, in Chapter 7, a wide range of
technological options which are directly related to crop
production in drought. This chapter is predicated on the
assumption that the first and most direct influence of
drought on the agricultural industry will be a reduction of
crop production over a wide area and that most other effects
stem in sequence from this first impact. The technologies

described in this chapter are those which can be used to increase the capture of rainfall for storage in the soil and
reservoirs, those which can be used to decrease the loss of
stored soil water or water stored in impoundments, those
which can be used to increase the amounts of water which
reach the soil either by irrigation or by precipitation enhancement and those which can be used to effect an increased
water use efficiency in crop production (more plant produced
per unit of water consumed).

The specific technologies described are terrace and contour farming, strip cropping, stubble mulch farming, minimum
tillage, use of windbreaks of various kinds, irrigation and
supplemental irrigation and weather modification. Plant
breeding as a means of adapting plants to the stresses imposed by drought is discussed as well as the application of
biophysical principles as a guide to agronomic practice and
to plant breeding for drought-proofing agricultural crops.
The message of this chapter is that advanced technologies and
general advances in agricultural research can, together,
greatly improve the resistance of our cropping systems to
losses in productivity which follow upon drought.

In Chapter 8 Dr. A. Berry Crawford of the Western Governor's Policy Office, Institute for Policy Research, has
organized current information on the responses of the state
and federal governments to the 1977 drought. Dr. Crawford
summarizes the geographical extent of the 1977 drought as
viewed from the perspective of the late summer of 1977. The
impacts of the drought, both agricultural and urban, which
have been reported through effectively coordinated state and
federal offices is also summarized. Dr. Crawford gives us
a "blow by blow" review of the early state-level activities
prompted by the drought. He shows us how, beginning in
February of 1977, the state and federal governments began to
communicate and coordinate efforts. This detailed accounting
of responses during 1977 is particularly useful since, as
suggested above, it tests the validity of the analyses and
predictions which were our 'best thinking' and presented with
some confidence at our symposium in February of 1977. Crawford's report also provides some cause for optimism that, at
least in the political realm, relatively rapid action is
possible when information is quickly brought to political
administrations which desire to act.

Dr. Steven H. Schneider's paper Forecasting Future
Droughts: Is It Possible? has been chosen as the final chapter as a reminder that, whatever the weather may be when
the reader picks up this symposium volume, there are droughts
in our future. Dr. Schneider lets us know that our ability

to anticipate future droughts, or even to judge whether the
drought of the 1970's is over, is severely limited and that
the prospect for improved skill at predicting drought in the
near future, at least, is not bright. Droughts are repeated
features of many different climatic regions and these regions are not totally unattached in terms of the climatic
processes which influence them.

Yet another perspective is added to the problem of
drought by Dr. Schneider who comments upon the fact that a
warming of the earth's climate is anticipated if the CO_2
concentration of the atmosphere continues to rise. Such a
warming may influence the general circulation features of
the atmosphere and hence the occurrence of droughts, particularly in the monsoon belts and the mid-latitude granary
regions of the world. Society, Dr. Schneider concludes, had
best continue to plan for climatic events such as droughts
since they are probable,if not yet forecastable.

The Denver symposium on American Droughts was exciting
for the speakers and the listeners. I hope some of the
reason for this excitement carries through the more formal
printed page.

1

History of
American Droughts

L. Dean Bark

Droughts have plagued man for centuries, undoubtedly
causing some of the famines referred to in the Bible. On
our continent, tree-rings indicate many early droughts including the "Great Pueblo Drought" from 1276 to 1299(3).

Today, as this symposium begins, newspapers are head-
lining drought conditions along the West Coast and in the
Northern Plains. Our concern is heightened by the realiza-
tion that the demands for food by the world's population is
rapidly approaching our ability to produce it. We know that
a serious drought in the food-producing areas of the world
could be catastrophic for mankind. Our great interest in
drought is indicated by a 236-page bibliography of articles
on the subject(10).

To set the stage for other topics to be covered in this
symposium, I have been asked to review the history of
droughts in North America. The task is difficult because
there is no universally applicable definition of drought.
Those of us associated with agriculture and food production
tend to be concerned with sufficient moisture to meet the
demands of growing crops. Much of our food is produced in
regions characterized by Thornthwaite (14) as sub-humid or
semi-arid. He points out that the position of the boundary
between those two classifications (which normally runs along
the 100th meridian) varies from year to year due to the
large variability of precipitation in this region. Thus,
droughts are a recurrent feature of the climate of the
Great Plains.

Others from more populated regions of the country are
more concerned about urban water supplies when considering

Contribution 129-A, Department of Physics, Agricultural
Experiment Station, Kansas State University, Manhattan, KS.

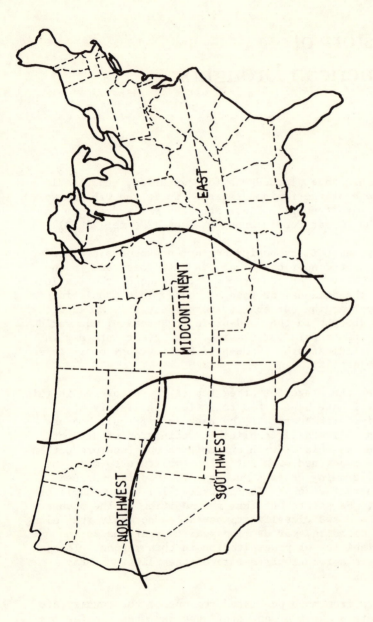

Fig. 1. Physical drought region of the United States as described by Warrick (16).

drought. In earlier times, these regions were in the humid
East. Now, the shift in population to the arid Southwest and
California has made the nation even more vulnerable to the
effects of urban droughts. The increased use of irrigation,
primarily in the arid and semi-arid regions, makes agriculture a competitor with cities and industries for limited
water supplies.

What is a drought? Many definitions are given in the
classical book by Tannehill (13) and a recent World Meteorological Organization Technical Note (18). I don't intend
to provide a definition in this short presentation. However,
I would like to point out that the variety of definitions in
use has made it somewhat difficult to know just when we have
had droughts in America. I'm not sure that much progress is
being made in this area.

Warrick (16) divided the continental United States into
four physical drought regions (Figure 1), citing important
physical characteristics, agricultural activity, and duration
of drought as the basis for classification. Drought could be
defined differently in each region. It is logical to extend
the boundaries of these regions northward into Canada and
southward into Mexico. Drought results from a widespread
circulation pattern in the atmosphere that does not respect
international boundaries.

Since the Midcontinent region is a transition zone
between the humid East and the arid Southwest, droughts are
a regular feature of the climate of this region and most of
our discussion will be on droughts occurring in this
section. Tannehill (13) reported only two droughts in the
East and called them "astounding occurrences". Of course,
his book was written before the severe drought of the
1960's in the Northeast.

The 1930's have become the standard for defining
drought. Most of us either experienced it first-hand, or
have heard our parents describe the hardships of the
"dirty-thirties" so that we feel we were there. You have
also seen the many poignant photographs taken for the Farm
Security Administration to document the period [Frontis-
piece and (5)]. At least we know Steinbeck's Grapes of
Wrath which describes conditions so eloquently that it is
easy to forget that not all droughts have been as devastating. The term "Dust Bowl", originating in the 1930's, still
hangs as the sword of Damocles over the economy of southwestern Kansas, and the Texas and Oklahoma Panhandles. Every
year as the spring winds start to move the soil in this region, the Nation watches to see if this is to be the year

that the Dust Bowl fulfills its destiny.

Many think that, in terms of general suffering, the 1930's were unique and that there will never be another drought like it. Others, particularly our journalistic friends, seem to anticipate that every dry spell will send clouds of dust swirling around the Empire State Building and the "Okies" will again head westward along Route 66, or its Interstate succesor.

The search for drought cycles has tended to confuse the historical account in my opinion. Droughts have been manufactured to "fit" cycles. Now, I am not saying that a particular year was arbitrarily categorized as a drought; however, it does appear that uniform criteria for including or excluding particular dry periods generally are not applied. Short-period droughts or those occurring only at a single weather station are difficult to include and arbitrary decisions must be made to handle these occurrences.

Very little is known about droughts in North America before the Civil War. Weather observation stations west of the Appalachians were few and widely scattered before 1860. Even today, long weather records in Mexico and northern Canada are not available. Tannehill (13) indicates that the second quarter of the 19th century was a period of deficient rainfall, and many parts of the country are known to have been dry near the middle of the century. I will discuss droughts in three categories: (1) Prehistoric, (2) Historic, and (3) Recent. Prehistoric droughts are those that occurred before Europeans settled the land. Historic droughts are those that have been documented in the journals, diaries, and newspapers of early settlers. The establishment of a network of stations for regular observations of weather has provided data to document conditions of recent droughts.

Prehistoric Droughts

The earliest records of drought in North America are those painstakingly derived from analyses of the growth-rings of trees. A. E. Douglass and his followers at the Laboratory of Tree-Ring Research at the University of Arizona have done pioneering work in this area. Fritts (3), from that laboratory, has suggested a model for the physiological relationship causing ring-width growth to correlate with variations in climate, and has provided a statistical evaluation of the relationship (3). Chronologies of tree-rings that extend back as far as 500 A.D. have been constructed for some locations. Fritts presents these data as departures from averages for 10-year periods for locations in the western United States. Although there is evidence of many localized droughts, he reports that wide-spread droughts occurred in 1576-1590, 1625-1635, 1776-1785, 1841-1850, 1871-1880, and 1931-1940.

Tree-rings have also been studied in other parts of North America. However, these studies are not as extensive in the drought-prone Midcontinent region. Weakly (16) identified prehistoric droughts from studies of tree rings in Nebraska (Table 1). Weakly also presents the duration of each period and the number of years between droughts. He reported that 12 droughts lasted for ten years or more, and three of them for more than 20 years. The drought that began in 1276 lasted 38 years. It is staggering to contemplate just what effect such a drought would have today. Douglass also identified droughts in the Pueblo Region at about that time (from 1276 to 1299) that were catastrophic to many of the Pueblo civilizations. Weakly did not find sufficient

Table 1. Drought periods identified from tree-ring analyses in Nebraska (Weakly, 17).

Beginning year	Ending year	Duration of period	Years between occurrences
1220	1231	12	
1260	1272	13	29
1276	1313	38	3
1383	1388	6	33
1438	1455	18	16
1493	1498	6	38
1512	1529	18	13
1539	1564	26	10
1587	1605	19	23
1626	1630	5	20
1668	1675	8	38
1688	1707	20	13
1728	1732	5	21
1761	1773	13	29
1798	1803	6	26
1822	1832	11	25
1858	1866	9	25
1884	1895	12	18
1906	1913	8	10
1931	1940	10	17
1952	1957	6	11
	Average	12.8	23.9

regularity in his wet-dry patterns to define a drought cycle. However, it seems clear that droughts have been a feature of our climate for thousands of years.

Historical Droughts

Moving forward on the time scale, the diaries and journals of early explorers and settlers provided some information on droughts. (1, 2, 8, 9, 12, 13). Coronado explored northward as far as Kansas in the mid-sixteenth century. However, his men were not particularly well qualified to describe and assess what they saw. Unfortunately, there was no climatologist in that expedition. There were comments in their journals on the large diurnal extremes of temperature and on some violent storms, but the treeless plains and the large herds of bison apparently captured most of the attention of Coronado's expedition.

It wasn't until the purchase of the Louisiana Territory in 1803 that an effort was made to describe the area and to assess its value to the new Nation. Unlike Coronado, who came north from the arid southwest, explorers, soldiers, and fur traders came from the humid east to the Louisiana Territory. Their descriptions, based on previous experience, can be misleading. Someone moving from the humid east to the semi-arid Plains might well consider a normal year to be desolate beyond comprehension. It is now clear that there is a difference between aridity and drought (6, 18) but it was not appreciated then.

Captain Zebulon Pike's assessment (1) of the mid-continent region in 1810 was that "in time it may become as celebrated as the sandy desert of Africa". The explorer, Stephen H. Long, apparently agreed, for in 1822 he wrote that the land was "almost wholly unfit for cultivation and, of course, uninhabitable by a people depending on agriculture for subsistence". Such expressions may indicate that these explorations, in the early years of the 19th century, were made during periods of drought (refer again to Table 1). Certainly the landscape and continental climate were unlike those that Pike and Long had previously experienced. Others shared the view of these early explorers and maps prepared of the area identified the region as "The Great American Desert". It was taken for granted that this desert would serve as a barrier to westward expansion.

Lewis (7) credits William Gilpin with changing the image of this region from "Great American Desert" to the "Great Plains." Gilpin was a prolific writer and speaker who devoted much of his energy to selling the Great Plains as a

desirable place for settlement. There were many others besides Gilpin and Pike who took opposing views on the value of
the broad area between the mountains of the East and those of
the West. History is spiced by repartee between the
"Boomers" and the "Gloomers." Malin (9) quotes many Kansas
newspaper accounts of this battle of wits that illustrate
that historical accounts of weather conditions are not un-
biased.

> "Enough has already been written about the 'dry
> year', 1860, both by those who exaggerate and those
> who denied its calamities, but we must berate the
> wicked folly of those who speak of that season as
> though it might be repeated, whenever dust flies
> for two or three successive days."
>
>   The KANSAS SPIRIT, 1872

There is no question but that the drought of 1860 made a
lasting impression. There were other years just before, and
after, 1860 that were also droughty to a lesser degree.
Eastern Kansas was just being settled then and the hardship
was too much to permit many to maintain their fragile existence. The drought of 1860 also affected Missouri, Iowa,
Minnesota, Wisconsin, and Illinois. Unfortunately, there
were few rain gauges installed then. The 1860 drought had a
pronounced effect on the settlement of Kansas and for years
"Gloomers" were concerned that every short dry-period would
lengthen into another 1860. The "Boomers" took the position
that the drought of 1860 could never recur. The result was a
distortion of climatic history in which droughts were often
denied, and the area was represented to be much the same as
the East.

> "A few years ago, at this time of the year we were
> cursed with disagreeable, suffocating and provoking
> sand storms. Sometimes they would last for several
> days in succession. We firmly believe we shall have
> none of consequence this spring. The climate is
> surely improving."
>
>   The Salina JOURNAL, March 1, 1877

Of course, it was also the fashion in those days to use the
press to campaign for a worthwhile cause. A little later in
the same year, in Abilene (a town near Salina), the editor
wrote:

> "Tuesday was by all odds the most disagreeable day
> of the season for dust . . . It insinuated itself
> through cracks and keyholes in clouds. Abilene

should have a street sprinkler when the campaign
opens next spring, and thus escape the annoyance.
We believe every business man would hail its advent
with pleasure and give it substantial support."

Abilene CHRONICLE, August 31, 1877

Other newspaper accounts from the work of Malin (9) contain some attempts to look on the light side of the climatic
shortcomings of the area:

"Last Friday evening was the most breezy of the
season. It was unsafe for small men with loose
fitting clothes to be on the street . . . Several
persons had so much gravel blown into their eyes,
that after the manner of unfeeling characters in
novels they now regard everything with a stony
gaze."

Medicine Lodge CRESSET, April 2, 1880

"Last Sunday the Kansas Zephyr was again abroad in
the land, and a reasonable quantity of the dry and
dusty land was aboard the zephyr. It resembled
when in good view of the same, across a newly plowed
field, or upon a well traveled road, the pictures of
a simoon in the desert of Sahara, as depicted in the
geographies. The Kansas zephyrs are a promiscuous
and pleasant (?) thing, they are. Real estate takes
its biggest rise during these times."

The Newton KANSAN, February 24, 1876

As you can see, it is difficult to know how we might decide
the intensity of these early dry periods, since the descriptions were more often than not written for purposes other
than climatic description. G. W. Martin, writing in the
Junction City UNION August 1, 1874, commented on conditions
in the year known in Kansas and Nebraska as the "Grasshopper
Year":

"Misfortunes never come singly, and a 'dry
spell' brings with it any number of disasters
and inconveniences. A drought nourishes chinch
bugs, sun-strokes, grasshoppers and profanity."

Following the Civil War, extensive anti-desert public-
ity by the western railroads finally established the Great
Plains concept. Rainfall was plentiful from the mid 1860's
to the mid 1880's in this area. Immigration into the
Plains area by farmers proceeded rapidly.

It was common to attribute the change in climate to the increased cultivation. Thornthwaite (15) quotes Samuel Aughey's text on physical geography and geology of Nebraska as follows:

"It is the great increase in absorptive power of the soil, wrought by cultivation, that has caused, and continues to cause an increasing rainfall in the state. After the soil is broken, a rain as it falls is absorbed by the soil like a huge sponge. The soil gives this absorbed moisture slowly back to the atmosphere by evaporation. Thus year by year as cultivation of the soil is extended, more of the rain that falls is absorbed and retained to be given off by evaporation, or to produce springs. This, of course, must give increasing moisture and rainfall."

"Rain follows the plow," became an accepted way of thinking Railroad advertisements for land sales often carried this theme [see Saarinen (11) for illustrations of such advertisements].

I cannot help but think of what a great job Madison Avenue might have done with that slogan for a TV commercial. A good selling job was done on Congress which passed the Timber Culture Act in 1873 in the belief that trees would increase rainfall sufficiently to eliminate climatic hazards to agriculture. Abundant rainfall in the Great Plains from 1875 to 1886 was a convincing argument that the goal had been accomplished.

It was a shock to discover that Mother Nature was still in charge, and not Congress, when rainfall again decreased in the Plains in the late 1880's and early 1890's. The dry years culminated in complete crop failure in the Great Plains in 1894. Occupation of this semi-arid region had begun in 1885 when the area was actually sub-humid. Immigration turned to emigration as homesteaders returned eastward, or continued westward.

Table 2 lists the droughts identified in the historical record by Ludlum (8) and some of their consequences. It is difficult to determine the intensity of the earlier droughts. It is also likely that the drought conditions might have had an effect in a broader area than those mentioned since little of the continent was settled in Colonial times.

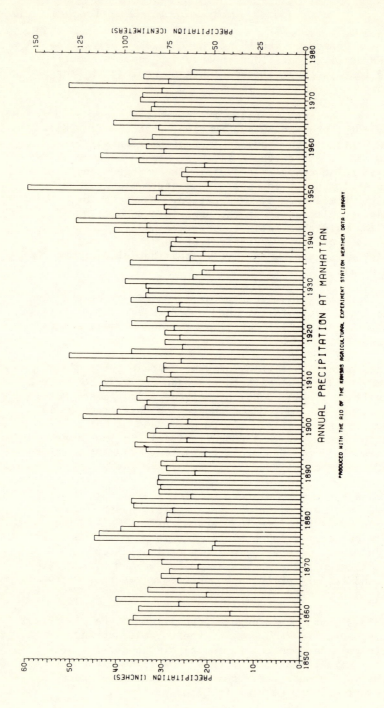

PRODUCED WITH THE AID OF THE KANSAS AGRICULTURAL EXPERIMENT STATION WEATHER DATA LIBRARY

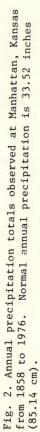

Fig. 2. Annual precipitation totals observed at Manhattan, Kansas from 1858 to 1976. Normal annual precipitation is 33.52 inches (85.14 cm).

Table 2.   Historical droughts in the Continental United
States. (Ludlum, 8).

Year(s)	Area of occurrence, consequences, and effects
1621	Pilgrim's crops threatened first summer
1623	Another dry spell endangered corn
1749, 1761, 1762	Fields of grain in New England so dry they caught fire
1805, 1822	Very dry in Eastern States
1850-51	Rain in California 1/3 normal
1854	Crop failures, New York to Missouri
1860	Kans., Mo., Iowa, Minn., Wisc., Ill.
1862-64	Put an end to extensive cattle industry in California
1881-87	Coupled with severe winters in Great Plains
1888-92	Fully half of settlers in Kansas and Nebraska left the area
1893-95	Extreme drought in Great Plains
1910, 1911, 1913	Serious, but short-lived droughts
1930's	Great Plains eastward to Great Lakes
1950's	Great Plains to southeastern United States
1961-66	Northeastern United States

Recent Droughts

The establishment of a national weather service late in the 19th century has provided a climatic record to more adequately describe the intensity and areal coverage of drought conditions. The last six listings in Table 2 are documented in these records. A few weather stations existed at the time of some of the earlier occurrences, but it is difficult to know whether the deficit in precipitation at a particular station was a local condition or part of a large-area situation.

Figure 2 illustrates the problem by presenting the annual precipitation totals at Manhattan, Kansas, from 1858 to 1976. Normal rainfall at this station is 33.52 inches (85.14 cm) per year. The severity of the drought of 1860 is apparent because the annual total was only 15.13 inches (38.43 cm). However, 1966 is not remembered as a drought even though only 15.42 inches (39.17 cm) of precipitation fell. Clearly a drought is more than a deficit of precipitation; however, rainfall records provide a means of comparing drought situations at various places and at different times. In the paper which follows, means of objectively classifying drought severity are described.

There are many good summaries of recent droughts (1, 2, 4, 8, 12). The Midcontinent region (Fig. 1) experienced major droughts centered on the years 1892, 1912, 1934, and 1935. Actual beginning and ending dates of these droughts varied with location within the region. Droughts occurring in the 1890's and 1930's were accompanied by winds that produced devasting dust storms that turned day into night (4). Winds were not as strong during the droughts of the teens and fifties (1) and consequently dust storms were not as severe.

The drought of the 1930's extended into Canada where it was particularly severe in 1936. In the 1950's, drought was more severe in the southern part of the Midcontinent region and many locations reported the drought to be the most severe ever experienced. Improved dry-land farming techniques and a better economy lessened the effects of this drought. Although weather observations are lacking to document the extent, it is known that these droughts also affected the semi-arid regions of Mexico south of the Texas border.

The worst drought in the humid East region began in the Northeast in the early 1960's. This prolonged drought eventually affected an area extending from southeastern Canada to Washington, D. C. The greatest center of population in North America (with its high water requirements) was involved. Near the end of the drought, reservoirs for New York City were down to 25 per cent of capacity.

Hughes (4) reports that, "Drought returned to the Southwest in the fall of 1969 and visited southern Florida in the following year. Abnormally dry weather set in over southern Calfornia and parts of Arizona in late 1969, spread across New Mexico and west-central Texas by mid-1970, and over central and south Texas in the fall of 1970."

Drought conditions also returned to the northern Plains in the early 1970's. As we write this, the Far West and the Rocky Mountain regions are concerned that winter precipitation was short in 1976-77.

Summary

Painstaking analyses of the width of growth-rings of trees provide evidence that droughts have been a regular feature of the climate of North America as far back as 500 A.D. (3). The length of these periods of weather that had an adverse effect on growth varied considerably. Weakly (17) indicates that one such period lasted for 38 years.

The recurrence of drought does not appear to be sufficiently regular to provide a "Drought Cycle" pattern that can be used to predict future droughts.

Although there is much evidence that periods of dry weather plagued the early settlers, it is not easy to evaluate the extent and severity of these droughts. Most reports were made on the basis of limited experience in a single locality, or a trip or two to the area of interest. It was not until homesteaders settled the Plains that it was possible to get a comprehensive view of the climate. Even then, particularly gifted writers, (and ungifted ones who owned newspapers) exerted undue influence in "shaping" the climatic image of the Plains. Accurate assessment of the climatic resources of the country had to await the establishment of a network of rainfall and temperature observation stations after the Civil War.

Since the establishment of observational networks, climatic records have provided a more objective method of identifying droughts. Droughts have occurred in the Midcontinent region at approximately 20 year intervals since weather records were started in the United States. They have also occurred in other regions of North America, but not as frequently nor with the regularity that they do in the Midcontinent region.

There is still no completely satisfactory criteria for identifying and describing droughts. There are often non-meteorological factors that are important in determining the economic effect of a rainfall deficit.

History clearly shows that drought is a feature of the climate of North America, particularly in the large Midcontinent region. Since there is no reason to think that our climate has changed significantly, we must learn the lessons of history to reduce the effects of drought on our way of life.

References Cited

1. Borchert, J. R. 1971. The dust bowl in the 1970's. Annl. Assoc. Am. Geog. 61:1-22.

2. Flora, S.D. 1948. Climate of Kansas. Kans. St. Board of Agric., Topeka, Ks. (pps. 123-127).

3.   Fritts, H. 1965. Tree-ring evidence for climatic changes in western North America, Mon. Wea. Rev. 93:421-443.

4.   Hughes, P. 1976. Drought: The land killer. American Weather Stories, U.S. Dept. Comm. NOAA-EDS, Washington, D. C. (pps 77-87).

5.   Hurley, F. J. 1972. Portrait of a decade, Louisiana State Univ. Press, Baton Rouge, LA.

6.   Landsberg. H. E. 1975. Drought, a recurrent element of climate. In Special Environmental Report No. 5, World Meteorological Organization. Geneva, Switzerland.

7.   Lewis, G. M. 1966. William Gilpin and the concept of the Great Plains Region, Anni. Assoc. Amer. Geog. 56:33-51.

8.   Ludlum, D. M. 1971. Weather Record Book. Weatherwise, Inc., Princeton, New Jersey.

9.   Malin, J. C. 1946. Dust storms, 1850-1900. Kans. Hist. Quart. 14.

10.   Palmer, W. C. and L. M. Denny 1971. Drought Bibliography. NOAA Tech. Memo. EDS 20. U. S. Dept. Com., U.S. Govt. Print. Office, Washington, D. C.

11.   Saarinen, T. F. 1966. Perception of drought hazard on the Great Plains. Dep. Geo. Resh. Pap. No. 106, University of Chicago.

12.   Special Assistant to the President for Public Works Planning 1958. Drought, A report on drought in the Great Plains and the Southwest. U.S. Govt. Print. Office, Washington, D. C.

13.   Tannehill, I. R. 1947. Drought: Its causes and effects. Princeton Univ. Press, Princeton, New Jersey.

14.   Thornthwaite, C. W. 1941. Atlas of Climatic Types in the United States, 1900-1939. U.S. Cons. Ser. Misc. Pub. No. 421. U.S. Govt. Print. Office, Washington, D. C.

15. Thornthwaite, C. W. 1941. Climate and the settlement of the Great Plains. In Climate and Man: Yearbook of Agriculture U.S. Dept. Agric., Washington, D. C. (pps 177-196.)

16. Warrick, R. A., P. B. Trainer, E. J. Baker, W. Brinkman 1975. Drought hazard in the United States: A research assessment. Monograph of Inst. of Behavioral Sci. University of Colorado, Boulder, CO.

17. Weakly, H. E. 1965. Agric. Eng. 46:85.

18. World Meteorological Organization 1975. Drought and Agriculture. Tech. Note No. 138, WMO No. 392, Geneva, Switzerland.

2

Drought: Characteristics and Assessment

Richard E. Felch

Introduction

At any time, drought is usually occurring somewhere in the world so that the economy of some nation or nations is being adversely affected. Our sumposium on North American drought was particularly timely because of the severe drought covering much of the United States. However, despite all of the problems drought has caused in the past, and its frequent occurrence, it is still poorly understood in terms of definition, man's ability to quantitatively describe and evaluate the severity of drought, and to some extent, the inability to react to drought conditions when they occur. The purpose of this paper is to point out some of the problems in defining and characterizing drought. The Palmer Drought Index serves as one means of quantitatively evaluating drought events, and thus particular attention will be directed to it in this presentation.

Drought is a meteorological phenomenon--an extended period of time with inadequate precipitation. However, its impact is often measured in terms of economic losses, yield and production cutbacks, all of which are compounded by other non-meteorological factors.

Most of the world's agricultural areas are subject to drought, but the duration and intensity vary greatly from one climatic zone to the next. Drought commonly remain unbroken for over a year, while on rare occasions droughts have continued with only negligible relief for nearly ten years. The impact of moisture deficiency is also dependent upon the timing and duration of the weather event, and the type of agricultural operation involved.

Drought and Aridity

It is important to distinguish the concept of drought
from the concept of aridity. Aridity is usually defined as
low average rainfall or available water, and it is a permanent climatic feature of the region. Drought, on the other
hand, is a temporary feature of the climate. In the context
of variability, drought occurs only when rainfall deviates
appreciably below normal. In this context, arid regions may
be less susceptible to drought than some areas of "heavy"
rainfall. This is particularly true from an economic standpoint because of the greater monetary investments in intense
agricultural areas.

Other weather events such as extreme temperature, low
humidity, high winds, and others can by themselves produce
drought-like conditions. The 1974 crop season in the United
States provides an excellent example. A very wet spring
delayed planting and early growth across most of the Corn
Belt. From mid-June to early July, conditions went from too
wet to extremely hot and dry, stunting crops and greatly
reducing yields, despite the fact that sub-soil moisture was
adequate in many affected areas. In the strict sense, a
drought event had not occurred, but it would be difficult to
convince farmers who lost their crops.

These brief comments emphasize the difficulty in developing a single definition of drought which will adequately
describe any of the myriad of situations that arise. The
requirements of definition depend on both the situation and
the person involved with the problem, whether he be a meteorologist, a statistician, a hydrologist, or an agriculturalist.
Several years ago the American Meteorological Society (3)
proposed the following definition of drought: "that drought
is a period of abnormally dry weather sufficiently prolonged
for lack of water to cause serious hydrologic imbalance in
the affected area." The definition further stipulates that
the term "should be reserved for periods of moisture deficiency that are relatively extensive in both space and time."

Many definitions from an agricultural standpoint are
based on the adaptability of the husbandry practices to the
"average" conditions since the operation must be adapted to
the rainfall characteristics of the region. Fitzpatrick (2)
defined agricultural drought as a state of deficient moisture
conditions which produce a lasting adverse effect upon
plants—particularly those of economic importance.

Some Drought Characteristics

The beginning and ending times of a drought are often rather vague, particularly the onset of a drought which often cannot be dated within two months. Droughts develop over a period of time. Palmer (5) has considered this problem in developing his drought analysis procedure and has devised criteria for objectively determining the end of drought periods.

Drought, in the agricultural sense, does not necessarily begin with the cessation of rain, but rather when available stored water in the soil cannot meet the evaporative demands of the atmosphere. The ability of a plant to transpire under conditions of limited soil moisture depends on the environmental demand and the availability of moisture to the plant, which in turn, depend to a considerable extent on the characteristics or degree of activity of the plant. Normally a plant extends its root system horizontally and downward as it grows, bringing a greater volume of soil within its sphere of influence. During a dry period roots may extract all available water from a soil volume, but if new roots can penetrate adjacent moisture-charged regions, transpiration can continue, although not at a maximum rate.

Drought is a regional manifestation of a generally fluctuating climate associated with a persistent aberration (abnormality) of the atmospheric circulation. These meteororlogical abnormalities can be explained in terms of (1) the physical forces and restraints which determine large scale atmospheric circulation patterns, coupled with (2) regional and local factors which superimpose local climatic peculiarities on the large scale climatic background. However, by far the greatest factor in the prolongation of drought is the absence of large scale vertical motion.

The areal extent of drought ranges from "small area" to so-called "continental droughts". Areas can range from a few hundred square kilometers to hundreds or thousands of square kilometers. A few generalizations can be made (9):

(a) It is almost impossible to get very severe droughts in a very small area.

(b) The average coverage of severe large continental droughts is about 2300 to 4200 kilometers in diameter.

(c) The more severe a large continental drought, the larger the area involved.

(d)   The larger the area involved, the greater the
range in soils, vegetation, and topography.

Thus, any means of describing drought must be versatile
enough to provide accurate answers over a large area. Numerous attempts have been made to develop indices which might
accomplish this task. This paper will not attempt to discuss
these in detail; however, a few comments and generalizations
will be considered.

Finally, some drought events may be relatively short-
lived and intense. The "sukhovei" winds of the Soviet Union
produce a veritable "atmospheric drought". This phenomenon
occurs when very dry air, intensified by high winds and
temperatures sweep northward from the southern deserts. The
extremely low atmospheric humidity causes severe damage
because the plant is unable to meet atmospheric demand. The
sukhovei may persist from less than a day to several days.
The availability of soil moisture becomes very critical in
determining the effect or extent of damage (1). "Sukhovei"
conditions also occur in North America (6).

Some General Thoughts on Drought Indices and Their Use

The major purpose for developing a drought index is to
provide a means for summarizing and periodically disseminating
drought and crop moisture information on a regional basis.
This type of information is needed by government agencies and
other groups having wide regional or national interests or
responsibilities. An example is those governmental agencies
which report crop progress and/or production prospects.

Such indices also provide additional information.
Specific examples of these will be discussed later in the
paper, but they include a basis for historical evaluation of
the likelihood of specific droughts occurring. This may be
used for regional and national planning as well as a guide to
the individual grower on the feasibility of a particular
agricultural operation. In addition, an adequate index would
provide a means for quantitatively establishing a basis for
evaluating the severity and intensity of drought, and
allowing for a fairer and more reasonable system for providing
drought assistance.

Opponents of such indices feel that the problem is much
too complex to take full account of all the pertinent physical
and biological factors. But one must take scale into consideration. No index is adequate to evaluate a particular crop
on a particular soil at a particular time. Even if such an
index were available, the instrumentation and data require-

ments likely would not be manageable. However, a field-by-
field evaluation is not required to develop a reliable and
informative index of drought.

The Palmer Index

The Palmer Index is one means of describing periods of
abnormally wet or dry weather. The Index combines precipitation and temperature data as predictor variables. The Palmer
Index has proven to be a reliable and accurate index for
evaluating the moisture situation and its impacts on crops.
It is, in the strictest sense, a measure of meteorological
drought. Palmer also developed the Crop Moisture Index to
evaluate the current moisture supply status in relation to
moisture demand. The two indices complement each other to
form very useful tools for monitoring the regional or
national agricultural production picture.

The Palmer Index is widely adaptable because it takes
into account the normal weather for each area. Using a
climatological analysis of long records of temperature and
precipitation, five constants are calculated which define the
moisture characteristics of the region of interest. Using
these constants, persistently normal weather in terms of
temperature and precipitation data produces an index value
of zero in all seasons in any climatic region. Further, an
extended period of extreme dryness (based on long historical
records) produces an index value of around -6, regardless of
the degree of aridity in the region. Although the Index was
developed for assessing drought, it demonstrates or evaluates
extremely wet situations equally well. Therefore, for the
last three years, the Index has been referred to as the
Palmer Index rather than the Palmer Drought Index.

No attempt will be made in this paper to present the
calculations for the Index. The method is described in some
detail in the U. S. Weather Bureau Technical Paper No. 45
(4). However, a few other points should be made. The Index
can be calculated on either a weekly or monthly basis.
Drought generally develops over a period of time. Similarly,
a drought is not necessarily ended by even a few heavy rains.
A prolonged period of above normal moisture is required to
refill soil profiles, reservoirs, and water tables.

This leads to another point. If an area is experiencing
unusual dryness, there are situations where the rain that
does fall is adequate to keep the top levels of the soil
moist and meet most of the moisture demand. The Crop Moisture
Index is useful here because it concerns itself only with the
amount of the moisture demand which can be met using current

Figure 1a

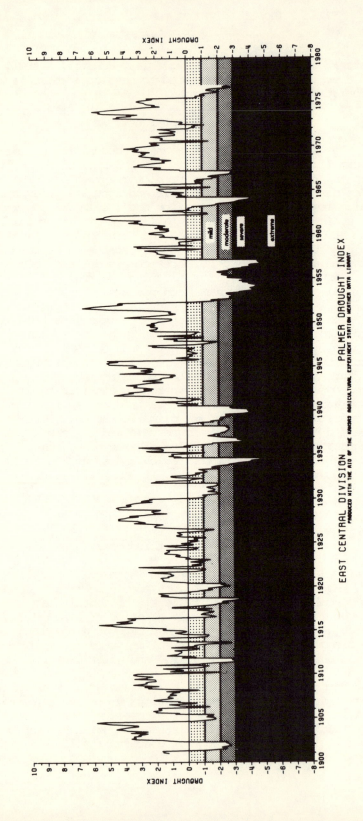

EAST CENTRAL DIVISION   PALMER DROUGHT INDEX
PRODUCED WITH THE AID OF THE KANSAS AGRICULTURAL EXPERIMENT STATION WEATHER DATA LIBRARY

Figure 1b

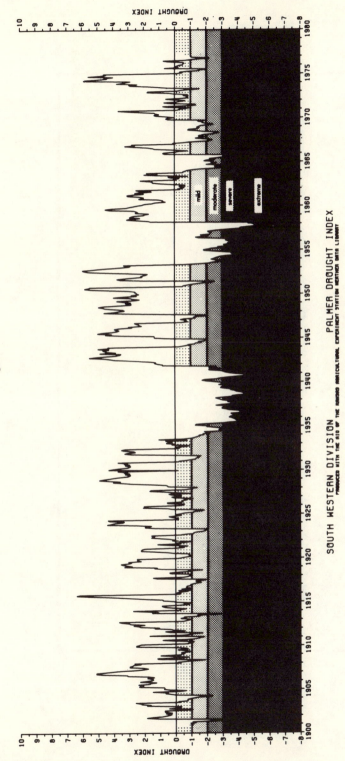

FIGURE 1.   Time series values of the Palmer Index for the period 1900
             to 1976 for the east central and southwestern divisions of
             Kansas. (Weather Data Library of the Kansas Agricultural
             Experiment Station.)

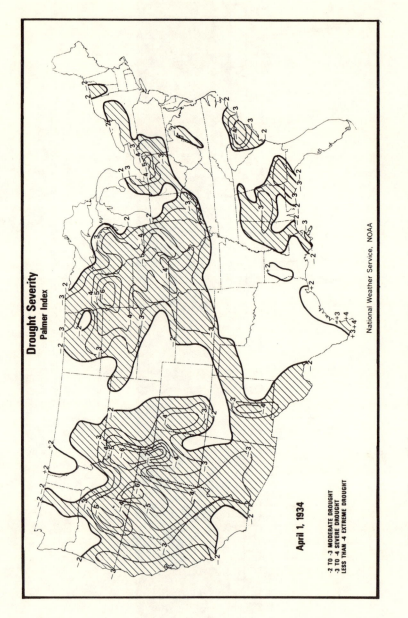

Drought Severity
Palmer Index

April 1, 1934

-2 TO -3 MODERATE DROUGHT
-3 TO -4 SEVERE DROUGHT
LESS THAN -4 EXTREME DROUGHT

National Weather Service, NOAA

Figure 2.   Palmer Index values showing drought development as of
April 1, 1934 (8)

supplies. While the overall soil moisture situation may be precarious, it is possible for crops to develop almost normally. Precarious is probably the appropriate word because with no soil moisture in reserve, crops can deteriorate very rapidly if rainfall ceases or returns to normal.

The Palmer Index also has its shortcomings. The calculations assume that a soil profile must be completely filled before runoff can occur. The Thornthwaite procedure (4) used to estimate evapotranspiration also has its limitations. Despite these and other problems, the Index has proven to be relatively stable and reliable over a number of years and a wide range of weather and agricultural situations in the United States.

Palmer Index Applications: Examples

Historical Analysis

It is often difficult to compare quantitatively one drought to another or even specify when drought conditions did occur. Through an index such as Palmer's, it is possible to calculate a long series of values based on historical data. Figure 1 was prepared by Dr. Dean Bark of Kansas State University and shows a historical series of calculated Palmer Index values for the east central and southwestern division of Kansas. From such a data series, evaluations may be of the likelihood of droughts occurring of varying intensities. It also shows some of the characteristics of drought, especially the tendency for persistence. For example, of the 13 occurrences of drought values greater than -2 in the east central division, 12 persisted for at least two years. The longest period of drought occurred in the 1950's. The 1930's drought was broken, briefly, in 1938, although this relief did not occur in the southwest division.

Such information is also useful in evaluating the way in which droughts develop. The area in which a drought begins can be identified. The spread and movement of the drought areas can also be monitored. This information can then assist in determining the agricultural potential of an area.

Patterns in Drought Development

Figures 2, 3, and 4 trace the development of the 1934 drought. On April 1, 1934, moderate to severe drought already existed across many parts of the country. Note that this pattern was very similar to early 1977. (See Figure 8)

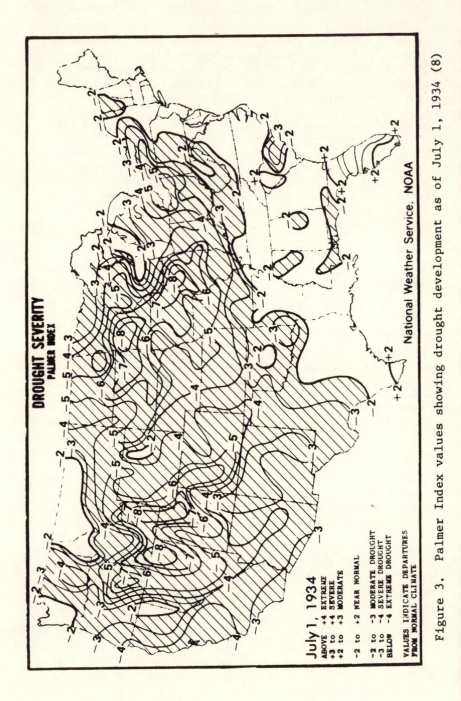

Figure 3. Palmer Index values showing drought development as of July 1, 1934 (8)

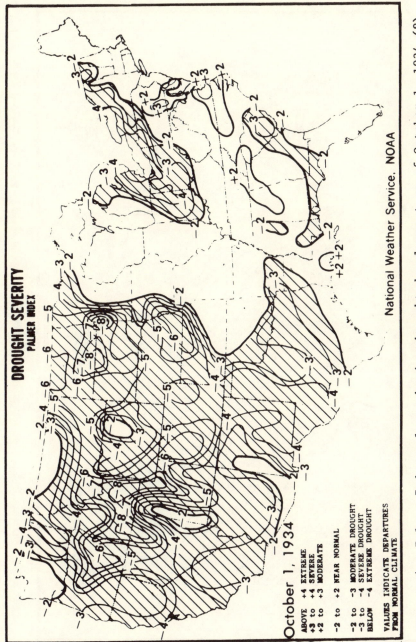

Figure 4. Palmer Index values showing drought development as of October 1, 1934 (8)

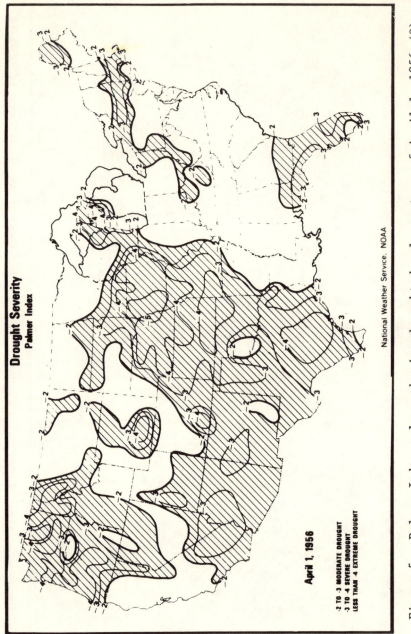

Figure 5. Palmer Index values showing drought development as of April 1, 1956 (8)

Exceptionally dry spring weather intensified the situation. By July 1 nearly the entire Country was involved except in South, Southeast, and Northeast. Values of -6 to -8 described the western Corn Belt, the northern Great Plains, and the Inter-mountain region.

By fall there was considerable improvement in the eastern half of the Country, but the Great Plains and western States showed little or none. Through the study and analysis of such maps and data it is possible to follow the development and intensification of the drought, as well as its termination. It is also possible to visualize the scope and coverage of the drought. The effects of drought on the Plains States and the "Great Dust Bowl" are still talked about today. However, 80% of the U. S. land area experienced at least moderate drought in 1934.

Figures 5, 6, and 7 document drought conditions in 1956. In certain areas the drought had continued six to eight years. Severe drought (-3 to -4) covered most of the central and southern Great Plains. The drought intensified through the summer months and into the fall. Ironically, it finally broke in 1957 with a year of very wet weather, serious flooding, and numerous other problems caused by too much moisture.

Another important feature of this series is the regionality. The drought situation in the 1950's was not as widespread or intense as 1934. Also it only seriously affected the southern half of the States. The 1930's generally hurt the northern two-thirds of the country. Thus, the central Plains were severely affected in both decades. If one is attempting to evaluate any possible cyclical behavior, it is important that the overall situation be kept in perspective.

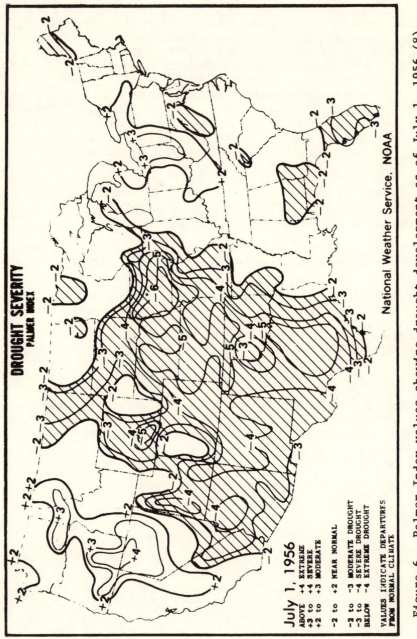

Figure 6. Palmer Index values showing drought development as of July 1, 1956 (8)

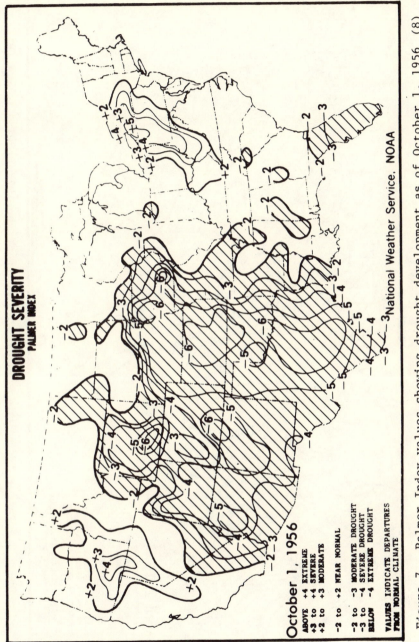

DROUGHT SEVERITY
PALMER INDEX

October 1, 1956

ABOVE	+4 EXTREME
+3 to	+4 SEVERE
+2 to	+3 MODERATE
-2 to	+2 NEAR NORMAL
-2 to	-3 MODERATE DROUGHT
-3 to	-4 SEVERE DROUGHT
BELOW	-4 EXTREME DROUGHT

VALUES INDICATE DEPARTURES
FROM NORMAL CLIMATE

National Weather Service. NOAA

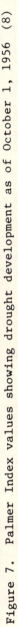

Figure 7. Palmer Index values showing drought development as of October 1, 1956 (8)

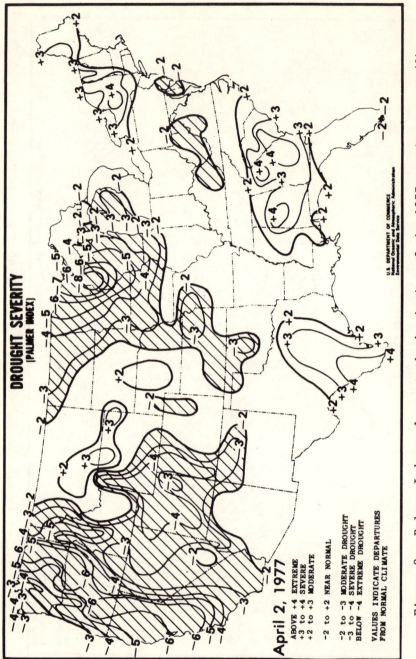

Figure 8. Palmer Index values at the beginning of the 1977 growing season (8)

Summary and Conclusion

Other papers in this symposium deal with the problems of the impacts and responses to drought. Since drought is a meteorological phenomenon, how may the meteorologist help avoid or alleviate its effects. There are two ways which have already been tried over many years with some degree of success. The first is the forecasting of the onset or cessation of drought and since this is a long period problem, obviously success does not come easily. The other is the planning of resources to make the best of the inevitable vagaries and circumstances of climate; this is best handled on a cooperative basis with experts from other disciplines such as agriculturalists, hydrologists, conservationalists, etc. It is an area which still requires a great deal of work. The crash programs of numerous States in response to the drought of 1977 clearly demonstrates the need for such an effort.

References

(1) Dzerdzeevskii, B. L. ed 1957. Sukhoveis and Drought Control. Akademiya Nauk SSSR. Institut Geografi. Translated by Israel Program for Scientific Translations, Jeruselum 1963.

(2) Fitzpatrick, E. A. 1953. Probability analysis of rainfall factors in drought (NSW), Rural Bank of NSW, Australia cited in Subrahmanyam, V.P. Incidence and Spread of Continental Drought, Report No. 2, Reports on WMO/IHD Projects, World Meteorological Organization, 1967.

(3) Huschke, R. A. 1959. Glossary of American Meteorology, American Meteorological Society, Boston, Massachusetts.

(4) Palmer, W. C. 1965. Meteorological drought. U. S. Department of Commerce, Weather Bureau, Research Paper No. 45, 1965.

(5) Palmer, W. C. and L. M. Denny. 1971. Drought Bibliography. U. S. Department of Commerce, NOAA Technical Memorandum, EDS 20.

(6) Rosenberg, N. J. 1972. Frequency of potential evapotranspiration rates in central Great Plains. Proc. Amer. Soc. Civil Engineers, Volume 98: IR2: 203-206.

(7) Thornthwaite, C. W. 1948. An approach toward a rational classification of climate. Geographical Review 38: 55-94.

(8) Weekly Weather and Crop Bulletin. 1976. A series of historical maps were published in Vol. Nos. (1976). U. S. Department of Commerce/Agriculture, Washington D.C.

(9) World Meteorological Organization. 1971. Assessment of Drought. An unpublished report of the Working Group on Assessment of Drought established by the WMO Commission for Agricultural Meteorology as Doc. 22, CAgM-V, October 1971.

3

Drought Impacts on American Agricultural Productivity [1,3]

James E. Newman [2]

Introduction

The purpose of this paper is to characterize the long
term variability and trends in grain crop production in North
America. Since 94% of all exports in the world grain trade
are from North America, as estimated by Brown (1), this
subject is a very relevant one, not only to the U.S. and
Canada, but to the world as a whole as well.

Agricultural production is usually considered the total
production of both food and fiber for any geographical area
or nation. On a worldwide basis the major portion of the
food energy consumed by Man comes from the cereal grains and
oil seed crops, commonly known as the commodity trade grains.
In the U.S. and Canada a greater consumption of animal products makes food energy from these commodity trade grains more
indirect than in most other areas of the world.

[1] Presented at the 143rd annual national meeting of AAAS,
Denver, CO., Feb. 21, 1977.

[2] Professor of Agronomy and Climatology, Dept. of Agron-
omy-Geosciences, Purdue University, West Lafayette, IN.
47907.

[3] Journal Paper No. 6812, Agricultural Experiment Station,
Purdue University, West Lafayette, IN. 47907.

The geographical limits of agricultural production, under dryland cultural practices, are largely controlled by either precipitation or temperature or both (2). This is certainly true when considering the climatic impact on the total agricultural production of the U.S. and Canada. Further, the main commodity trade grains of wheat, corn, soybeans, sorghum, and barley are produced under dryland cultural practices for the most part. Many of these production areas are in semi-arid to sub-humid climatic regions. The fact that these production areas are so located makes drought or the lack of timely precipitation the chief climatic risk.

Corn production is largely determined by land area, technical input and seasonal growing conditions. Land area and technical input are management decisions that are controlled by farmers. However, seasonal weather conditions are not controllable under dryland cultural practices. Since about 90% of the commodity trade grain crops in North America are produced under dryland cultural practices, seasonal weather and climatic fluctuations bring about most of the annual variability in production. The leading seasonal weather or climatic fluctuation associated with negative deviations in national production is <u>drought</u>.

Drought has been defined in many different ways. These differences in definition are usually associated with a specific interest or purpose. An economist may define a drought as any water shortage that produces an adverse effect on an established economy. An agricultural drought is normally confined to the shortage of soil moisture in the rooting zone of crops, while a hydrological drought relates to below normal levels in ground water, natural lakes, man-made reservoirs, and stream flows. A meteorological drought is best characterized by an abnormally low precipitation anomaly over a prolonged period, usually over a large geographical area, producing agricultural drought as well as hydrologic changes in water supplies.

In this analysis drought is considered as a negative deviation in precipitation on a time and space scale large enough to produce a negative impact on the national agricultural productivity of the major commodity grain crops of wheat, corn, soybeans, sorghum and barley.

Data and methods

The basic data used in this study were obtained from the annual reports published by the Statistical Reporting Service (SRS) of the U.S. Department of Agriculture (USDA) and Agricultural Statistics published by Agriculture-Canada. Average national yields in bushels per acre, adjusted to harvested acres, were used in all cases possible. National production statistics on these major commodity crops are rather consistent and comparable over the past 50 years in both the U.S. and Canada.

Applied statistics provides three common measurements of variability. These are the standard deviation, the mean deviation and some expression of the range in the variability of the individual samples. Among relative measurements of variability there are also three expressions: (1) the standard deviation divided by the sample mean, (2) the mean deviation divided by the sample mean, and (3) the median divided by the range. In the following analyses the mean, the standard deviation and the "coefficient of variability" (CV), an expression of the standard deviation divided by the mean, were calculated as routine outputs from the data bases.

The first step in these trend analyses on North American crop yields began with the fitting of a fourth degree polynomial curve to data on annual national average crop yield as illustrated in Fig. 1 for U.S. wheat. The fourth degree values of Fig. 1 are:

$$Y = -32.57154492 + 1.19574466X - 0.00854797X^2 - 0.00000088X^3 + 0.00000013X^4$$

where Y = yield in bushels per acre and X is year. This procedure was developed by Dr. E. McCloud, Professor of Agronomy, University of Florida, and applied in "Impact of Climatic Fluctuations on Major North American Food Crops" (3). From this curvilinear regression procedure annual national mean yield trends were established for U.S. corn, wheat, soybeans, and sorghum, plus Canadian wheat and barley. The actual annual national yield deviations in bushels per acre from these regression yields were used to calculate a standard deviation for any run of years desired, thus minimizing any changes in yield trend for the period. Coefficients of variability were calculated from the standard deviation over the mean where the mean was determined by curvilinear regression for the time period concerned.

The overall period of years used in the previously described procedures was 1866 to 1975 for the U.S. corn and wheat crops, 1924 to 1975 for the U.S. soybean crop and 1929 to 1975 for the U.S. sorghum crop. For the Canadian wheat and barley, years 1921 to 1975 were used in both cases.

Eleven-year moving averages were calculated and are illustrated in Figs. 2, 3 and 4 for the U.S. wheat crop. The

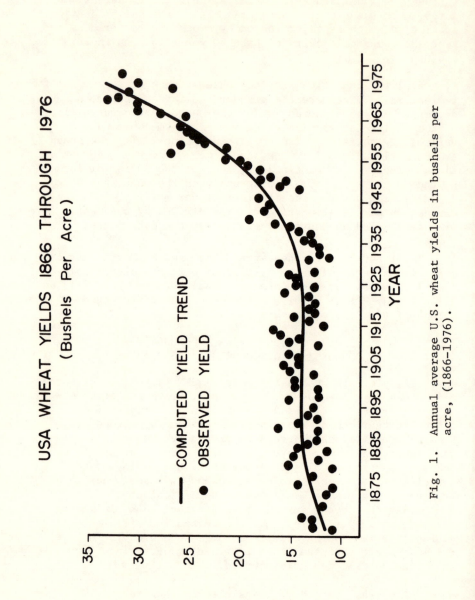

Fig. 1.   Annual average U.S. wheat yields in bushels per
          acre, (1866-1976).

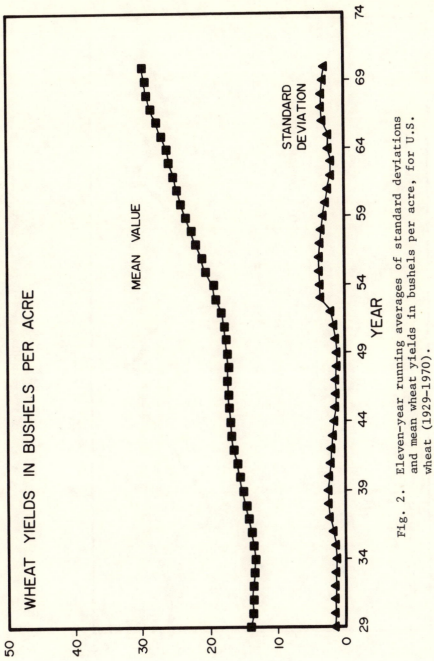

Fig. 2. Eleven-year running averages of standard deviations and mean wheat yields in bushels per acre, for U.S. wheat (1929-1970).

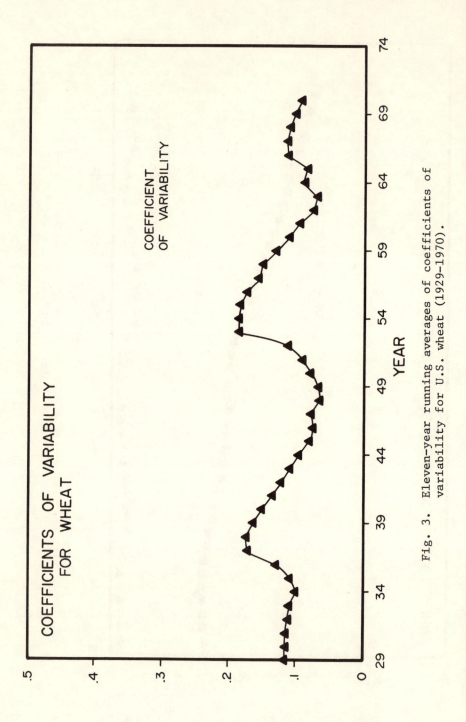

Fig. 3. Eleven-year running averages of coefficients of variability for U.S. wheat (1929-1970).

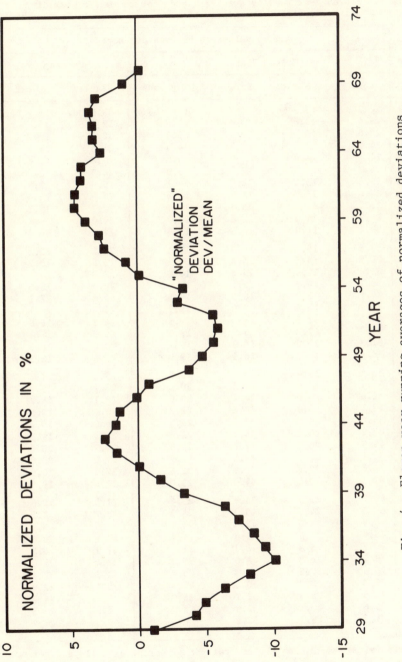

Fig. 4. Eleven-year running averages of normalized deviations from the mean for U.S. wheat in percent, (1929-1970).

Table 1. Eleven year running average yields for the major commodity
grain crops of North America.*

Year	United States				Canada	
	Corn	Wheat	Sorghum	Soybeans	Barley	Wheat
1929	24.2 bu.	13.9 bu.		13.1 bu.	23.6 bu.	16.7 bu.
30	24.4	13.6		13.6	22.7	15.8
31	23.6	13.6		13.9	22.3	15.7
32	24.0	13.5		14.5	21.5	14.8
33	24.4	13.4		15.2	20.8	13.8
34	24.7	13.3	12.7 bu.	15.9	20.3	13.1
35	25.6	13.5	12.6	16.1	19.9	12.8
36	26.6	13.7	13.4	16.6	20.6	13.4
37	27.2	14.0	13.6	17.0	20.2	13.1
38	28.1	14.3	13.6	17.3	22.0	14.4
39	29.4	14.9	14.3	17.8	22.4	14.4
1940	30.6	15.3	15.0	18.1	23.2	15.1
41	31.5	15.7	15.3	18.4	23.6	15.3
42	32.8	16.3	15.8	18.6	23.8	15.8
43	33.7	16.8	16.1	18.9	24.0	16.3
44	34.5	16.9	16.9	19.1	24.4	17.1
45	35.2	17.0	18.0	19.1	24.2	17.1
46	36.1	17.1	18.5	19.5	24.3	16.8
47	36.7	17.2	18.3	19.8	25.0	17.1
48	37.3	17.0	18.3	19.7	26.2	18.3
49	38.1	17.2	18.7	19.9	25.5	18.1
1950	39.4	17.4	18.6	20.0	25.2	17.7
51	40.4	17.6	19.2	20.3	25.1	18.2
52	42.6	18.0	20.4	20.6	26.1	19.2
53	43.5	18.9	22.1	21.3	26.0	19.3
54	45.0	19.2	33.7	21.5	26.6	19.7
55	47.2	20.3	25.2	21.6	26.9	19.9
56	49.7	20.9	27.2	21.9	27.7	20.6
57	52.1	21.8	29.5	22.2	27.2	20.0
58	54.1	22.4	31.9	22.6	27.2	20.0
59	57.3	23.2	34.0	23.0	27.4	19.9
1960	60.1	23.9	36.9	23.4	27.5	19.6
61	63.1	24.5	40.3	23.9	28.7	20.5
62	65.9	25.0	42.8	24.1	30.0	20.9
63	68.9	25.6	45.0	24.4	29.9	20.4
64	70.7	25.9	46.7	24.7	31.2	20.8
65	73.7	26.8	48.0	25.0	32.4	21.6
66	78.9	27.5	49.3	25.4	33.7	22.4
67	79.3	28.3	50.8	25.6	35.1	22.9
68	79.6	28.9	52.1	25.9	37.0	24.2
69	79.6	29.1	52.3	25.9	37.7	24.5
1970	81.7	29.5	52.9	26.4	37.5	24.2

*Yearly values computed on the central (6th) year of each 11-year period.

moving averages were generated by starting with a given 11-
year period of annual values, then dropping the first year
value and replacing it with the next in the sequence. The
results are plotted on the middle, or 6th year. The time
period used for this analysis was the 50-year period of 1924
to 1974 in all cases except the U.S. sorghum crop. Annual
national average yields for sorghum are available from 1929
to 1974, thus reducing the 11-year running average analysis
to a 45-year period. These procedures generated 11-year running averages from 1929 through 1970 for all North American
grain crops except sorghum which began in 1934 due to data
series limitations. The resulting values are reported in
Tables 1, 2 and 3.

My reasons for confining the running change analysis to
the past 50 years are threefold: (1) the computed yield
trend could be divided between the period of annual increases
in trend yield related to changes in technological inputs
from an earlier period of little or no change in mean annual
national grain yield trends; (2) more uniformity was evident
in the statistical procedures used in making these annual
estimates; and (3) the data were available on the major commodity trade grains. Other multiple-year running averages
were computed including 5-, 7-, 9- and 10-year periods, but
the 11-year period was selected for the following reasons:
(1) odd-year running averages have the advantage of producing
a truly middle year in the time period and (2) the 11-year
period gave the lowest difference in the sums between positive and negative deviations from the time-trend mean yield
as determined by the 4th degree equation procedure applied in
Fig. 1.

The 11-year running averages for normalized deviations
illustrated for U.S. wheat in Fig. 4 are based on the mean of
the deviation from the trend mean for each year and then
averaged over the 11 years, where the trend mean is computed
from the same 11 years. However, the trend mean for any
given 11-year period was determined from a curvilinear regression fit to a 46-year period for the U.S. sorghum crop,
to a 51-year period for U.S. soybeans and to a 110-year period for U.S. corn and wheat crops. In the case of Canadian
wheat and barley the regression curve fit covers 54 years.

Results and discussion

Before about 1930 annual yields for the major North
American grain crops were essentially static. Since then a
series of technological advances has caused yields of major
commodity grain crops to double and, in some cases, to
triple.

Table 2. Eleven year running average coefficients of varability for the major commodity grain crops of North America.*

Year	Annual CV values in percent					
	United States				Canada	
	Corn	Wheat	Sorghum	Soybeans	Barley	Wheat
1929	11.6%	11.7%		11.4%	18.6%	26.8%
30	11.2	11.5		12.4	19.8	27.8
31	12.9	11.5		11.3	19.6	28.0
32	14.2	11.2		11.9	21.5	32.0
33	14.6	11.0		15.3	20.4	37.3
34	16.0	10.1	18.7%	17.7	18.0	34.3
35	16.7	10.9	18.4	16.6	14.7	28.7
36	16.8	12.9	21.7	15.2	14.7	30.4
37	19.4	17.1	23.3	15.1	13.7	29.8
38	20.2	17.3	23.6	14.5	25.9	37.8
39	19.7	16.4	25.6	11.7	25.9	37.9
1940	16.1	15.1	20.1	10.2	24.3	36.0
41	16.0	13.5	19.0	10.4	22.8	34.8
42	14.1	12.2	16.0	8.4	22.4	33.0
43	13.6	10.9	15.8	9.2	20.9	28.8
44	13.0	9.6	18.2	10.3	19.5	25.8
45	12.7	8.1	16.0	10.8	20.4	21.2
46	11.4	7.6	13.5	9.6	20.3	20.9
47	11.8	7.9	13.8	9.2	21.5	22.2
48	12.1	6.6	13.8	9.6	22.3	25.5
49	11.5	6.7	13.0	9.2	18.7	24.2
1950	11.1	8.0	13.0	8.9	19.3	26.1
51	12.0	9.2	12.2	8.5	19.2	27.0
52	13.2	11.3	16.9	9.4	19.5	26.4
53	11.6	18.5	24.7	7.7	19.7	20.0
54	13.5	18.5	28.2	8.2	17.1	24.0
55	14.4	18.4	32.5	8.6	16.5	23.2
56	16.7	17.4	36.2	9.7	13.7	20.0
57	17.4	15.7	36.1	9.9	16.1	24.4
58	18.7	15.0	33.1	9.9	16.1	24.4
59	17.5	13.1	29.1	7.4	16.9	24.0
1960	17.1	11.1	27.2	6.1	17.1	23.5
61	15.7	9.6	23.7	4.4	17.2	20.2
62	16.1	7.5	18.4	3.3	19.4	22.2
63	15.1	7.0	15.2	4.3	19.3	21.7
64	15.3	8.6	13.9	5.5	18.0	21.2
65	13.0	8.5	11.5	5.7	18.0	21.5
66	12.1	11.3	10.1	5.9	18.2	21.2
67	13.6	11.4	11.1	6.5	18.3	21.5
68	13.2	10.6	10.8	6.5	12.0	12.6
69	12.7	10.2	10.4	6.9	10.8	11.7
1970	10.5	9.4	8.3	6.2	11.1	12.0

* Yearly values computed on the central (6th) year of each 11-year period.

Table 3. Eleven year running average deviations from mean yield trend for the major commodity grain crops of North America.*

Year	United States				Canada	
	Corn	Wheat	Sorghum	Soybeans	Barley	Wheat
1929	- 6.2%	- 1.0%		-2.4%	+ 1.2%	+ 6.2%
30	- 6.4	- 4.2		-2.3	- 1.5	+ 2.1
31	-11.2	- 4.9		-4.2	- 2.2	+ 3.1
32	-11.2	- 6.4		-3.0	- 4.9	- 2.2
33	-12.1	- 8.3		-0.8	- 7.9	- 8.7
34	-12.1	-10.2	- 8.4%	+0.8	- 9.5	-13.9
35	-12.6	- 9.4	-11.8	+0.8	-11.3	-17.0
36	-10.2	- 8.6	- 7.2	+0.6	- 7.7	-11.0
37	- 8.0	- 7.5	- 6.4	+0.8	- 9.4	-13.0
38	- 7.8	- 6.4	- 6.1	+0.9	- 0.8	- 4.7
39	- 6.4	- 3.4	- 1.1	+0.7	+ 0.6	- 5.0
1940	- 3.8	- 1.7	+ 3.3	+2.0	+ 3.8	- 1.1
41	- 2.0	- 0.6	+ 5.1	+1.9	+ 4.7	- 0.8
42	- 1.5	+ 1.6	+ 8.0	+2.2	+ 4.8	+ 1.2
43	+ 0.8	+ 2.5	+ 9.0	+1.7	+ 5.0	+ 2.9
44	+ 0.4	+ 1.6	+11.6	+1.8	+ 5.8	+ 6.4
45	+ 0.5	+ 1.3	+14.6	+1.3	+ 3.7	+ 4.7
46	+ 0.6	+ 0.5	+14.3	+0.3	+ 3.3	+ 2.1
47	+ 0.8	- 0.8	+10.1	+1.1	+ 4.7	+ 2.1
48	+ 2.5	- 3.8	+ 5.9	-0.8	+ 8.0	+ 6.7
49	- 3.8	- 4.8	+ 2.8	-1.4	+ 4.1	+ 4.2
1950	- 4.7	- 5.7	- 3.5	-2.1	+ 1.6	+ 0.6
51	- 4.5	- 6.0	- 6.6	-1.7	- 0.4	+ 1.2
52	- 5.2	- 5.6	- 7.4	-1.9	+ 1.7	+ 5.0
53	- 3.1	- 3.0	- 6.4	-0.2	- 0.1	+ 3.9
54	- 4.3	- 3.4	- 6.2	-0.3	+ 0.4	+ 4.0
55	- 4.3	- 0.2	- 6.8	-1.1	- 0.2	+ 3.2
56	- 2.9	+ 0.8	- 6.4	-1.0	+ 0.8	+ 4.9
57	+ 1.1	+ 2.3	- 5.1	-1.0	- 2.8	+ 0.8
58	+ 2.1	+ 2.8	- 3.6	-0.9	- 4.8	- 1.3
59	+ 2.3	+ 3.8	- 3.5	-0.4	- 6.3	- 3.2
1960	+ 4.3	+ 4.6	- 1.4	-0.4	- 8.0	- 6.7
61	+ 5.6	+ 4.6	+ 1.7	+0.6	- 5.5	- 3.6
62	+ 6.7	+ 4.1	+ 2.6	+0.3	- 3.0	- 2.9
63	+ 7.4	+ 4.0	+ 2.7	+0.3	- 5.5	- 6.8
64	+ 8.1	+ 2.6	+ 2.2	+0.3	- 3.4	- 6.5
65	+ 7.1	+ 3.2	+ 1.1	+0.4	- 1.5	- 4.0
66	+ 7.6	+ 3.2	+ 0.5	+0.5	+ 0.2	- 1.8
67	+ 8.0	+ 3.4	+ 0.8	+0.4	+ 1.9	- 0.6
68	+ 7.5	+ 2.9	+ 1.4	+0.6	+ 4.8	+ 3.5
69	+ 4.4	+ 1.0	+ 0.3	+0.7	+ 4.5	+ 3.7
1970	+ 3.3	- 0.3	+ 0.9	+0.3	+ 1.9	+ 1.1

Annual deviations in percent

* Yearly values computed on the central (6th) year of each 11-year period.

Table 4. Estimates of annual crop yield variability*.

Crop species	Period of record	Mean yield**	Standard deviation	Coefficient of variability**
	Crop years	Bu/acre	Bu/acre	Percent
United States				
Corn	1866–1975	35.6	4.46	12.5
Wheat	1866–1975	16.5	1.70	10.3
Sorghum	1929–1975	28.5	3.80	13.3
Soybeans	1924–1975	20.1	1.50	7.5
Canadian				
Barley	1922–1975	27.4	4.50	16.4
Wheat	1922–1975	18.6	4.30	23.1

* From Impact of Climatic Fluctuations on Major North American Food Crops, The Institute of Ecology, Washington, D. C., 1976.

** Mean yields were determined by regression trend and the coefficients of variability were calculated from annual deviations from regression trend.

Table 5. Estimates of decadal changes in annual crop yield variability.

Crops	Decadal periods			
	1931–1940	1941–1950	1951–1960	1961–1970
	Coefficients of variability			
United States				
Corn	15%	10%	12%	8%
Wheat	14%	9%	10%	9%
Sorghum	20%	18%	24%	12%
Soybeans	12%	10%	8%	7%
Canada				
Barley	25%	17%	15%	12%
Wheat	35%	25%	18%	12%

Can these trends be sustained? Learned statements on this subject are both qualified and cautious. Most agronomists feel that present yield levels can be sustained but that future increases will come at a much reduced rate (4). Another view is that crop yields per unit area will level off or decline slightly, even with the continued additon of technology, because most new arable lands will be increasingly marginal. However, almost everyone agrees that the yield trend increases over the past two or three decades cannot be sustained on a national or continental basis (5).

Deviation from regression trends in annual yields are not random through time among the major grain crops of the North American continent. From examination of the running average analyses the deviations from regression yield trends follow a bi-decadal pattern for U.S. corn, wheat, sorghum and soybeans, as well as for Canadian wheat and barley, as is illustrated in U.S. wheat in Figs. 3 and 4.

However, these bi-decadal patterns or periods contain some inconsistencies. This is particularly true in the 1950's and 60's. A 1958 unpublished presidential report on "drought in the 1950's" shows the greatest intensity in the southern Great Plains area (6). Further, drought conditions in the 1950's did not develop northward into Canada. This results in the Canadian cyclic yield deviations lagging the U.S. crops somewhat in the running average analyses. Another aspect of these bi-decadal deviations is that negative deviations are greater in magnitude than are positive deviations. The positive normalized deviations of 11-year means are generally close to 5% and seldom more than 10% from regression trend and sustained over a longer run of years while negative deviations are often greater than 10% as is shown in Table 3, and illustrated in Fig. 4.

The positive and negative deviations from mean trend add up to approximately zero in most cases. There are some disagreements, particularly for U.S. corn and wheat. The reason for this lack of agreement may be related to the least-squares regression fit of the yield trends. For U.S. corn and wheat the regression curve fit time period was 1866 to 1975, instead of the last 50 years or so for all the other grain crops.

The results presented in Tables 4, 5 and 6 are based on two most commonly used statistical expressions of variability: the standard deviation expressed in absolute terms of bushels per acre and the coefficient of variation expressed in relative terms as percent of the standard deviation. The mean, standard deviation and the coefficient of variation for

the major North American grain crops are shown in Table 4.
The period of record relates to the continuous run of years
available data on annual national average yields based on
harvested acres.

In every measure of variability during the sample periods, the U.S. soybean crop is the lowest, thus making it the
most reliable crop from a national annual production viewpoint, among these major commodity grain crops. The Canadian wheat crop has the greatest year-to-year variability.
Among the major U.S. grains the sorghum crop is the most
variable. This high variability for U.S. sorghum annual
yields is likely related to the location of its main production area -- the southern high plains, where drought risk is
high in the absence of irrigation.

The decadal changes reported in Tables 5 and 6, using
10-year rather than 11-year moving average, for the U.S.
corn crop varied between 6 and 15% with 1931-40 (Table 5) the
highest and 1956-65 (Table 6) the lowest. The increase to
13% in the 1966-75 results from highly variable production
between 1970 and 1975. Much of this variability is related
to the climatic diversity of the geographical area covered by
the U.S. "Corn Belt". It is limited to the west and southwest by precipitation, to the north and northwest by temperature, and to the east and south by land resource limitations
related to topography, fertility and extremes in seasonal
rainfall distributions. All these geographical limitations
induce annual production variability each year in the broad
marginal areas around the "Corn Belt".

The annual production of U.S. wheat has the lowest variability among the cereal grains in North America. This low
variability is particularly striking when the U.S. crop is
compared to the Canadian wheat crop. Much of the increased
stability in the U.S. wheat crop is apparently related to the
much more climatically diverse production areas and the domi-
nance of the winter-type wheat. The annual production variability for U.S. spring wheat is similar to the Canadian crop
when computed alone. For the period 1924-75 the CV value for
the U.S. spring wheat crop is 19.7% compared to 23.1% for the
Canadian crop.

The lower variability of the Canadian barley crop compared to the wheat crop has two possible causes: (1) Barley
is the feed grain of Canada; therefore, it is grown over a
much broader area than wheat. (2) It is more tolerant to
low growing season temperatures; therefore, it is a lower
risk crop in the northern and more marginal production areas
of Canada.

It is evident, both from the 11-year running average analysis and the decadal change analysis presented in Tables 5 and 6, that variability has not been static over the past 50 years among the major grain crops of North America. A simple time series plot of national annual average yields reveals two types of yield variability: (1) year-to-year variability related to growing season conditions dominated by weather and (2) a curvilinear increase in yields over the past 50 years caused by the rather continuous addition of technological developments as is illustrated in Fig. 1 for U. S. wheat.

Placing some acceptable statistical estimates on these two distinct types of variability collectively over these past 50 years is not the difficulty. It is, rather, the inseparable interrelationships of the two.

It can be debated that changes in decadal variability as well as changes in the regression time-trend yields are caused by changes in technology or climate or both. However, it is clear that relative variability as represented by decadal changes in the coefficients of variation has decreased in recent decades as reported in Tables 5 and 6. During the same period, however, the absolute variability has increased from approximately 50 to 150%. This results from the rapid increases in total annual production. This relationship holds among all the major commodity crops of North America. Therefore, over the past four decades the relative variability among the major grain crops of North America has gone down. At the same time the absolute variability has increased. These comparisons are made in Table 7 for U.S. corn and wheat.

The reduction in relative variability among the major grain crops of North America is about 35% as estimated by decadal changes in CV values. This means that relative variability in year-to-year production has been reduced by about one-third over the past four decades. This reduction in variability is associated with the adoption of technology over the same period. The evidence for this conclusion is presented in Tables 5 and 6.

By calculating a linear regression for each decadal period separately, the reduction in variability increases rather continuously over the four decadal periods. But, the reductions in variability over the four decadal periods exist regardless of whether the regression technique used is confined to the individual decadal period or calculated over the entire four decadal periods.

Table 6. Estimates of decadal changes in annual crop yield variability.

Crops	Decadal periods			
	1936-1945	1946-1955	1956-1965	1966-1975
	Coefficients of variability			
United States				
Corn	11%	10%	6%	13%
Wheat	11%	8%	8%	9%
Sorghum	22%	21%	9%	8%
Soybeans	10%	9%	4%	6%
Canada				
Barley	24%	18%	14%	11%
Wheat	34%	25%	20%	11%

Table 7. Estimates of decadal changes in annual crop production variability.

Crops	Decadal periods			
	1936-1945	1946-1955	1956-1965	1966-1975
	Production variability			
United States				
Corn (CV%)	11%	10%	6%	13%
Production*	2406	2759	3602	4959 bus.
Variability*	264.6	275.9	216.1	644.7 bus.
Wheat (CV%)	11%	8%	8%	9%
Production*	864	1130	1197	1596 bus.
Variability*	95.0	90.4	95.8	143.6 bus.

* Total production and annual mean decadal variability in millions of bushels.

Table 8. Estimates of annual production variability among the major commodity grain crops for North America.*

Crops	Yield trend mean (1975)	Coefficient of variability 1966-1975	Annual variability			
			Deviations from predicted mean trend yields			
			1 in 2	1 in 3	1 in 5	1 in 20
				years		
United States						
Corn	6073	13%	395	789	1,184	1,578
Wheat	2126	9%	96	191	287	383
Sorghum	905	8%	36	72	108	145
Soybeans	1685	6%	51	101	152	202
Canada						
Barley	648	11%	36	72	107	143
Wheat	410	11%	23	45	68	90

* In millions of bushels.

Another possible explanation of the changes in variability among annual national crop yields over the four
decadal periods has been that of unusual occurrence of good
weather years. It is evident from the 11-year running average analysis, as illustrated in Fig. 3, that the interannual
variability of wheat yields was greater in the 1930's and
1950's than it was in the 1940's and 1960's. These decadal
changes are associated with a series of good and bad weather
years. But, the series of good and bad weather years is
somewhat out-of-phase between U.S. and Canada as determined
by positive and negative deviations in annual national yields
reported in Table 3 and Fig. 4. Therefore, the series of
good and bad years has limited validity as an explanation of
reduced variability when considered over such a large geographical area and over four decades of 1930's, 40's, 50's
and 60's. From such a time and space scale analysis, one can
conclude that technology has been the dominant factor in reducing the variability in annual U.S. and Canadian crop production over the past 50 years and that good and bad seasonal
weather has caused major decadal changes in crop yield variability. Further, the main difference between good and bad
seasonal weather has been the persistence of large scale
droughts in the mid-continental grain producing areas of
North America.

How large an annual production variability can be expected among these major commodity grain crops of North America?
Estimates of the magnitudes of these annual expected variations are reported in Table 8. For example, about once in
20 years U.S. corn production can be expected to deviate by
1.6 billion bushels or more from normally expected national
production because of annual growing season conditions.
These estimates are based on the probability of occurrence
over the past 45 to 50 years. The magnitude of these annual
expected deviations in total national production among the
major commodity crops agrees rather closely with USDA Statistical Reporting Service estimates made with similar assumptions.

Summary

Caution must be exercised in the application of the
estimated probability values for expected deviations from
mean value trends. From the 11-year running average yield
analyses presented here, good seasonal weather years and bad
seasonal weather years do not occur at random in time or
space. Historically, they have occurred over a series of
years roughly in alternate decades. Therefore, both positive and negative deviations in expected annual production
are likely to be additive over a series of years. From a

geographical standpoint, good and bad seasonal weather deviations have not occurred historically across all the North
American grain producing areas in the same year. Positive
and negative deviations in annual national grain production
have been grouped in an annual time series for given geographical production areas but this relationship does not
hold across all geographical production areas at the same
time historically. Therefore, it can be concluded that the
expected deviation in annual production among all the North
American grain crops will be <u>less than</u> the expected annual
production deviation of any single commodity crop or production area. Also, it is likely that deviations among all the
North American grain crops will not be all positive or all
negative across all production areas for the same year. This
is a most fortunate reality for the people of North America
and the world as well.

References

Brown, Lester R., The world food prospect, Science 190:1053-1059 (1975).

Newman, J. E. and R. C. Pickett, World climates and food supply variations, Science 186:877-881 (1974).

Impact of climatic fluctuation on major North American food crops, edited by A. Dexter Hinckley, published by the Institute of Ecology, 1315 16th Street N.W., Washington, D.C. 20036 (1976).

Thompson, L. M., Weather variability, climatic change and grain production, Science 188:435-441 (1975).

Living with climatic change, Proceedings of Toronto Conference Workshop, Science Council of Canada, 150 Kent St., Ottawa, Ontario, K1P 5P4 (1976).

Drought: A special presidential report, The White House, October (1958).

4

Drought:
An Economic Perspective

Roger F. Riefler

Like a hurricane, flood, earthquake, or tornado drought
is a natural disaster. Unlike these other crises, however,
drought, in a sense, represents a "non-event"; it is difficult to identify the onset of a period of prolonged drought
and it is likewise difficult to isolate the termination
point for a period of protracted drought. These complexi-
ties are reflected in the problem of defining drought. To
the meteorologist drought may connote a period of abnormally dry weather or lack of precipitation. To the geologist
or hydrologist drought is viewed in a broader perspective -
e.g. a sufficient lack of water, including surface and
ground water as well as precipitation, so as to cause a significant hydrologic imbalance in an area. From an even
broader perspective drought may be defined as a moisture
deficit in the physical or natural sub-system of an area that
has a significant impact on the human eco-system of that region or area. To view drought from an economic perspective,
this latter definition of drought must be accepted; it is
only when drought affects the human eco-system that is becomes an economic problem.

In the 1970's we have seen drought impinge significantly on two sub-systems of our overall human eco-system: the
agricultural sub-system and urban sub-system. The 1974 and
1976 droughts in parts of the Great Plains area illustrates
the former drought impact while the 1976-77 drought in California represents the latter (as well as the former). What
are the economic implications of prolonged drought? How
will they affect the agricultural and urban sub-systems of
our economy? In this paper we will focus on the agricultural sub-system for two closely related reasons. First, we
have more experience in the area of agricultural drought
impact. Second, much of the following analysis of agricultural drought impact can be applied, in only slightly modified form, to an investigation of the effects of drought on

the urban economy.

The study of drought should definitely be an interdisciplinary task given our current knowledge on the topic. The challenge to the climatologist is drought explanation and prediction. The challenge to the engineer, agronomist and other technologists is drought control. The challenge to the economist is assessing the economic impact of drought. To all scientists the need is to measure, predict and prescribe for drought impact. For the policymaker, either in the private or public sector, the objective is to respond effectively on the basis of accumulated knowledge.

From an economic viewpoint the problem of drought at first glance appears to be yet another "shortage crisis" similar to the energy crisis and the materials shortage so typical of the 1970's. Drought, like the energy crisis, curtails the supply of economic resources and, given demand, results in higher prices and diminished economic activity. As such, many of our available theoretical constructs or models, developed and applied over the 1930-1969 period, where concern was with underutilization of existing resources, no longer seem applicable in the "new world" of the 1970's. Our traditional policy palliations, based on these models, appear inoperative in the world in which we suddenly find ourselves. It is my objective in this essay to demonstrate that, although some change in emphasis and model design is necessary to adequately respond to the challenge of prolonged drought, the efficacy of existing theory and applied models remain when the goal is to explain and prescribe for the economic impact of serious moisture deficiency.

LEVEL OF ANALYSIS

Given our definition of drought as the significant impingement of a moisture deficit in the physical system on the human eco-system, any economic analysis of drought must first address the question of the level of the economy at which that impact is felt. Is the adverse impact of drought confined to the individual level or is it felt at the regional level, the national level, and/or the international level? An answer to this question is crucial to both our ability to assess the economic impact of drought as well as to our success in prescribing corrective policies.

Clearly agricultural drought affects the individual farmer or rancher. This follows directly from our definition of drought. What form does this impact take? Obviously a decline in physical output would be expected. Will this decline in production result in reduced income or will price increases or crop insurance cushion income fluctuations? If income declines will the result be to draw down previously accumulated wealth, increase indebtedness, incur bankruptcy, and/or to outmigrate? For the individual agriculturist, unable to control the demand for his output (e.g. as a "price-taker") adjustment to drought may take one of three forms: 1) supply adjustments (i.e. summer fallow, diversification, irrigation, etc.), 2) financial adjustments (i.e. draw down wealth, increase debt, insure), or 3) migration (either physically dislocate or find or increase nonagricultural activity). If drought impact is confined to the individual level, economic assessment and, most likely, economic policy should be "supply-oriented". Concentration is on the response of the supply side of the agricultural model (the farmer) to prolonged drought.

Once drought reaches regional proportions the measurement of economic impact becomes more difficult. But at the same time the adjustment potential of the economy increases as do the policy options available to decision makers. Even in an agriculturally-oriented region such as Nebraska, for instance, only 14% of current state earnings emanate directly from agriculture and another 6% from agricultural processing industries. Thus the number of agriculture-nonagriculture "trade-offs" increases presenting more options for the amelioration of drought impact. While the "openness" of a region, in terms of exporting a significant fraction of output and importing a large percent of needs, still dictates an emphasis on supply-side adjustment to drought, more degrees of freedom are available for demand-side adjustments and policy (e.g. public works projects in impacted regions).

As one goes up the spatial heirarchy to the national and international levels one more closely approximates a "closed" economy. In such a system the traditional supply/demand models of economic activity more adequately describe the impact of drought, the response of the economy to prolonged drought and the policy options available for ameliorating that impact. The importance of demand-side analysis and policy grows, not as a substitute for models emphasizing the supply-side, but as a complement to such research.

The parallel between the energy crisis and drought impact is indeed striking. Concentration at the individual level and generalization from the individual to society as a whole is easy and in both cases leads to rather pessimistic conclusions. Like the average American's love for the automobile and therefore the "locked-in" nature of the demand for gasoline, the individual's need for food products and the farmer's "locked-in" production possibilities result in a rather gloomy view of the problem at hand.

The burden of adjustment is placed on the supply-side and prospects do not appear promising. Further our traditional economic models, with their emphasis on demand determinants and manipulation, are poorly designed for the analysis of these issues.

The point of the above analysis, however, is that these four conclusions are not necessarily valid. Prolonged drought, like diminishing supplies of energy, are likely to impinge on the regional if not national and international economy. What is needed is not a new set of economic tools for measurement and policy purposes, but at most a shoring up of the supply-side of existing analytical techniques. A pertinent question remains, however. At what spatial level is the economic impact of future drought likely to occur? An answer to this question must entail an analysis of past drought occurrences and speculation as to future drought magnitude and duration.

HISTORICAL ANALYSIS

Susceptibility to drought in the United States appears greatest in the southwest and midcontinent portions of the country (26, pp. 15-27).[1] While other areas, such as the Northeast may undergo drought, (witness the 1961-66 drought), the probability of both short-term and especially long-term drought appear highest in the southwest and midcontinent regions. The historical record of the Great Plains in particular should therefore be helpful in assessing the appropriate spatial level of analysis for drought economic impact research

Droughts undoubtedly preceded white settlement of the Great Plains. The recorded history of the area shows four periods of prolonged drought impinging on the human eco-system: those occurring during the 1890's, 1910's, 1930's and 1950's. The latter two occurrences are especially well documented. While the 20 to 22 year cyclical nature of severe drought is intriguing from a predictive standpoint our current inability to explain the cause of these cycles precludes their use for firm forecasting purposes (see 26, p. 14 for alternative cycle theories).

The drought of the early 1890's significantly affected individual agriculturists in the Great Plains area decreasing output, income and resulting in significant spatial dislocation, (e.g. migration). Although records are sparse,

---

[1]The comparatively low level of urbanization in a majority of states in these regions, with exceptions such as California, suggest the emphasis of this paper on agricultural drought as opposed to urban drought.

drought undoubtedly led to regional instability as well as heavy outmigration. The relative high level of self-suf- iciency of the regional economy, however, probably indicated a low "multiplier" effect on total national income and em- ployment; the impact was felt primarily by the agricultur- ists and secondarily at the regional level. Although the relative impact on the regional economy was undoubtedly large, the low level of regional development indicates that the absolute magnitude of decline (by modern standards) was probably small. Settlement patterns, partly reflecting fed- eral land disposal policies, were responsible for the sever- ity of drought impact as well as for the outmigration re- sponse to adversity. Federal land policies, developed for more humid climates, resulted in farms which were too small, from an economic viewpoint, to facilitate adaptations to prolonged drought. Federal policies requiring the plowing of homesteads or, in later cases, their grazing further constrained the individual's adaptive flexibility to drought. It is doubtful, however, that the impact of the 1890's drought extended beyond the regional level.

The first drought of the twentieth century, centered on 1912, seems to have had a more limited adverse impact. While individual farmers were undoubtedly affected, develop- ments in dryland farming technology as well as previous moves toward increases in farm size must have helped to off- set the negative effect of drought. Increased agricultural prices resulting from World War I further helped limit the economic impact of drought. Impact was confined to the in- dividual farmer, mainly in terms of reduced physical output. The region was affected to a much lesser extent.

While agriculture suffered from depressed market con- ditions from World War I until the depression of the 1930's, farmers responded to economic adversity by increasing their output. Adequate rainfall, improved varieties of grain and advancements in farm machinery technology made expansion of output the preferred means to attempt to maintain income levels (as well as to pay off the indebtedness incurred to purchase machinery) in the face of falling prices. During this period we see the typical response of the Great Plain's farmers and ranchers: good years (with respect to precipi- tation) are taken as normal years and production is extended to marginal land.

The drought of the 1930's, extending from 1930-1939, but especially severe in 1934 and 1936, has been well documented in both the technical and popular literature. Response to lagging farm incomes in the 1920's made agriculture especial- ly susceptible to the onset of drought. The combination of

drought and national depression was staggering indeed. Depressed output and depressed prices in agriculture had severe
adverse impacts not only on farmers (income losses, bankruptcy), the region (outmigration, unemployment), but also
the nation. They key role of agriculture in the national
depression was emphasized by New Deal legislation and studies designed to reverse that condition. (1)

While the drought of the 1950's was comparable in climatic terms to that of the 1930's its economic impact was
much less severe (26, pp. 57-58). The adverse impact of
drought was confined to the individual and regional levels.
But even at these levels the adverse effect was offset by a
healthy national economy (and federal aid to agriculture
under policies dating from the 1930's).

The record for the 1970's is, of course, incomplete.
The evidence to date indicates drought conditions of relatively short duration in 1974 and 1976-77. While the 1974
drought was relatively concentrated geographically, the 1976-
77 drought has been widespread, extending from Michigan to
Colorado and from North Dakota to Oklahoma. Further west
1976-77 drought conditions extend from Montana to California.
As is usual for a non-event such as drought, identification
of the climatic dimensions and economic impact is difficult.
Research to date suggests individual impact has been significant but that the regional impact has been smaller than
the historical record would suggest (25).

What of the economic impact of future drought? Historical trends suggest a sanguine outlook. Given our increased
knowledge concerning the operation of the economy another depression such as the 1930's appears unlikely. We have the
knowledge to avoid a collapse in aggregate demand such as
occurred in that decade. If we are successful in maintaining a healthy overall economy, a task admittedly much more
difficult than avoiding a repeat of the 1930's, the worst we
might expect is a repeat of the 1950's experience-adverse
effect at the individual and regional level. Given the increased use of groundwater and surface streams for irrigation since the 1950's even these negative effects on individuals and regions may be cushioned. Increased farm size,
diversification, improved seed varieties and technology and
the increased importance of non-farm sources of income also
encourage a more optimistic viewpoint as to future drought
impact. These considerations suggest that the adverse effects of drought are likely to be concentrated at the individual and regional level. Measurement, assessment and
policy prescriptions must therefore focus on this level of
analysis. By necessity they will be largely supply-side or

"shortage" oriented in emphasis.

Several factors, however, cloud this essentially fav-
orable view of the economic impact of future droughts. First
and foremost we still see agriculturists taking the years of
good precipitation to be the normal years and planning ac-
cordingly. This tendency, when combined with the increased
capital intensity of farming activity (and concurrent increase in indebtedness) makes the individual agriculturist
more susceptible, economically, to prolonged drought. An
increase in absentee farm ownership may also reduce the
adaptability of agriculture to drought (4).

Secondly, recent changes in the structure of regional
economies may serve to magnify the effect of drought, initially confined to the agricultural sector, on the overall
level of regional well-being.[2] Increased local manufacturing
of farm implements and increased local processing of agricultural ouputs may, by means of linkage or interindustry effects, serve to multiply or magnify the original negative impact of declining farm income. Further as regional industrial structures as a whole approach that of the nation such
"multiplier" or indirect effects are likely to become larger;
as regions import less of their requirements these linkage
or indirect effects become larger and less spreading, in a
geographical sense, of adverse impact takes place.

Thirdly, while irrigation may ameliorate the impact of
short duration drought by evening out the "peaks and valleys"
of water availability as well as increasing yields, it is not
the final panacea for drought. Unrestricted use of groundwater for irrigation purposes during drought conditions may
severely deplete available supplies. Local groundwater
levels in Nebraska, for instance, were seriously depleted by
the 1974 drought (15). If, on the other hand, use of available water for irrigation purposes is rationed or otherwise
restricted, yields from irrigated land may fall. See (25).
In the case of prolonged drought, irrigation may alter the
time-phasing of economic impact, delaying its onset but extending its temporal duration, while not appreciably changing
its overall economic effect.[3] Increased competition for

---

[2]One of the prime advantages of input-output analysis, see
the following section, is to identify these changes in structure and assess their influence on the transmission of negative growth impulses such as drought.

[3]This extenuation could be caused by the necessity to replen-
ish acquifiers before obtaining pre-drought irrigation levels
and crop yields.

available water from industry, recreation and energy producers may even prevent this.

Finally, the decade of the 1970's has seen a growing
awareness of the crucial worldwide population/food supply
nexus. The effect of the 1972 Russian drought and resulting
purchases of U.S. grain products as well as the 1974 World
Food Conference in Rome have highlighted diminishing world
food reserves, increased population and a precarious food-
stuff balance. With approximately ten percent of the world's
population currently facing starvation and the increased importance of the United States as a supplier of foodstuffs
might not the impact of prolonged drought in the future extend beyond individual, regional and even national boundaries
to encompass the entire world? (See 17, 18 for such a view--
even in the absence of drought).

RAMIFICATIONS FOR ECONOMIC ANALYSIS OF DROUGHT

Based on historical trends as well as on our assessment of the current situation of the domestic economy it is
clear that to gauge the economic impact of drought we need
models of economic activity at the individual agriculturist's
level and at the regional level. National and international
analysis, while clearly subsidiary to individual and regional
analysis, is also indicated. The crucial issue, then, is
what form should our models take at each level.

The largest challenge is to understand the individual
farmer's response to a drought situation. This necessitates
a "supply-side" model of the adaptability of agriculturists
to changes in weather or hydrological conditions. A dynamic
or multiperiod programming model of decisions under risk
seems most appropriate here. Farmers tend to establish or
build their demand for resources on the basis of their experience during years of good moisture supply. Drought, however, necessitates adjustment. Thus existing ("normal practice") behavior cannot be used as a guide to response to
drought conditions. Adjustment to drought may take the
following forms: 1) conservation to available water (i.e.
changing cultivation practices-summer fallow), 2) water augmentation (i.e. irrigation), or 3) altering agricultural
practices (i.e. changing crop or livestock types, using
drought resistent varieties and diversification). While all
of the above responses are basically "technological" and
therefore amenable for inclusion in a single decision-mak-
ing model, an additional model is needed to determine the
financial flexibility of the farmer. He may also attempt to
adjust to drought by 4) financially spreading or sharing
drought related costs (i.e. insuring or maintaining crop or

cash reserves).

At the regional level existing models will either have
to be adapted for drought analysis or new models formulated.
Most existing regional models are demand-oriented. As mentioned above, given the "openness" of an agricultural region
such as the Great Plains, regional drought response is likely
to be largely supply-oriented. Existing conceptual frame-
works aimed at explaining population flows (i.e. migration)
and capital flows should, therefore, be directly applicable
to drought study. See for instance (8, 23, and 24).

Input-output models should be especially helpful in analyzing drought effects. Table 1 illustrates a typical input-output transactions or gross flows table. As a descrip-
tive construct the table utilizes the sales equals purchases
accounting identity: rows in the table capture the distribution of industry sales, labor services, imports and other
value added (e.g. taxes, depreciation) while columns in the
table show purchasing patterns by industry, households, exports and other final demand (e.g. government, investment
sectors of the regional economy). Applied at the regional
level, input-output analysis has the advantage of delineating
not only the structural composition of the economy - as measured by the gross output or outlay entries - but also the
linkages between or interdependency among the various sectors
of the local economy. Given the initial impact of drought
on agriculture, the analyst may wish to disaggregate agricultural producing and purchasing sectors to emphasize linkages in these areas. A further refinement of the basic model
would be to introduce a water production/consumption row and
column in the interindustry matrix to assist in measuring
water dependency rates. The flexibility of input-output models enable the analyst to adapt the basic model to the issue
under scrutiny.

In addition to the ability of an input-output model to
describe the interdependency of a regional economy and assess
the direct impact of drought, the model may be used to assess
the total or direct and indirect impact of drought on the e-
conomy. See Chenery and Clark (5) or Richardson (21) for the
assumptions and methodology used in such an analysis. Input-
output has been successfully applied in the context of "sup-
ply-constraint" problems. In the area of environmental economics see (21, Chap. 11). Work by Lamphear and Roesler (14)
on the impact of irrigation on the economic conditions in Nebraska and Holland (12), Hackbart, Hultman and Ramsey (9)
and Miernyk (19, 20) on the regional effects of the energy
crisis demonstrate the ability of input-output to assist in

From \ To	Purchasing Sectors				House-holds	Exports	Other Final Demand	Total Gross Output
	1	2	3	$\cdots$ n				
Producing Sectors 1	X_{11}	X_{12}	X_{13} $\cdots$	$\cdots$ X_{1n}	C_1	E_1	F_1	X_1
2								
3	Interindustry Transactions				$\cdots$	$\cdots$	$\cdots$	$\cdots$
$\vdots$								
n	X_{n1}	X_{n2}	X_{n3} $\cdots$	$\cdots$ X_{nn}	C_n	E_n	F_n	X_n
Labor	L_1	L_2	L_3 $\cdots$	$\cdots$ L_n	L_h			
Imports	I_1	I_2	I_3 $\cdots$	$\cdots$ I_n	I_h		I_f	
Other Value Added	V_1	V_2	V_3 $\cdots$	$\cdots$ V_n				
Total Gross Outlays	X_1	X_2	X_3 $\cdots$	$\cdots$ X_n				

X_{ij} = sales from industry i to industry j

TABLE 1: Input-output transactions

analyzing supply-oriented changes in a regional economy. Studies by Carter and Ireri (3, 13) and Davis (6, 7) use an interregional version of input-output analysis to specifically analyze water usage patterns and their economic impact or effect. Combining input-output with regional simulation models (18) or linear programming techniques (21) further facilitate analyzing the regional dimensions of drought.

At the national and international level existing (largely demand-oriented) models seem quite capable of handling an assessment of drought impact. At the national level, as the 1930's and 1950's droughts demonstrated, possibly the most important determinant of drought impact is the health of the overall economy. Existing models adequately gauge the health of the total economy as well as provide policy makers with the necessary information to ameliorate recession. However, further research on the price elasticity of demand for agricultural products (i.e. the response of quantity purchased to changes in price) clearly is needed. Such research, by emphasizing the liklihood of substitution in food consumption patterns, would facilitate an assessment of the flexibility of demand in adjusting to drought conditions. This demand flexibility, which must be analyzed at the national level, would complement the supply adaptability research at the farm level.

Analysis at the international level, like that at the national level, should be demand-oriented. Unlike national analysis, however, fixed consumption habits can be assumed to facilitate analysis. While high standards of income in the United States allow us flexibility in response to drought (i.e. we have the option of consuming more grain directly, as opposed to current practice of using grain stuffs to produce meat, thereby extending a drought diminished supply of grain), such an option is not available in much of the rest of the world. In the U.S. demand for a specific agricultural product depends on: 1) domestic population, 2) price, 3) income and 4) price of related goods. In much of the rest of the world living standards are such that factors 2-4 can be ignored. This simplifies international analysis of drought impact. A demand simulation model, such as refinement of that contained in (18), should adequately capture the international effects of prolonged drought as well as allow for an analysis of various drought response scenarios.

CONCLUSIONS

Drought, like so many economic issues we seem to be encountering in the 1970's, is initially a supply-side problem in the sense of causing a decrease in the amount of resources available to meet society's unlimited wants. But although initially a supply-side phenomena, to a significant extent, especially at the national and international level, its economic impact will be demand determined. As a corollary to this fact, it is likely that policies to soften the economic impact of drought must operate on both the supply side (i.e. better technology, aid to the farmer) and demand side (i.e. healthy national economy, substitution in consumption). The lesson is clear: an assessment of the economic impact of drought must look at both the supply and demand sides of the economy.

Given this fact we can be relatively optimistic concerning our ability to measure, analyze and prescribe for drought impact. While much work remains to be done, especially at the individual agriculturist and regional level, existing analytical techniques can be used or adapted to both assess impact and suggest ameliorative measures. What is needed is refinement of existing methods, not the evolution of a completely new set of theoretical and empirical models.

REFERENCES

(1) Braeman, J. undated. The dust bowl and the new deal.
     unpublished manuscript, University of Nebraska-Lincoln.

(2) Campbell, D. 1968. Drought, F. W. Cheshire, Melbourne.

(3) Carter, H. O. and D. Ireri. 1970. Linkages of Califor-
     nia-Arizona input-output models to analyze water trans-
     fer patterns, in A. P. Carter and A. Brody, eds.,
     Applications of Input-Output Analysis, North Holland
     Publishing Co. (pps. 139-167).

(4) Center for Rural Affairs. undated. Wheels of Fortune,
     Center for Rural Affairs, Walthill, Nebraska.

(5) Chenery, H. B. and P. G. Clark. 1959. Interindustry
     Economics, John Wiley & Sons, Inc., New York.

(6) Davis, H. C. 1967. A multiregional input-output model
     of the western states emphasizing heavy water-using
     sectors, unpublished Ph.D. dissertation, University of
     California, Berkeley.

(7) Davis, H. C. 1969. Interregional production and water
     resource dependencies among the western states. Western
     Economic Review 7:27-39.

(8) Greenwood, M. J. 1975. Research on internal migration
     in the United States: a survey. The Journal of Eco-
     nomic Literature 13:397-433.

(9) Hackbart, M. M., C. W. Hultman and J. R. Ramsey. 1976.
     On the economics of energy allocation. The Review of
     Regional Studies 6:98-108.

(10) Harschbarger, C. E. and M. Duncan. 1977. The economic
     realities of drought. Monthly Review of the Federal
     Reserve Bank of Kansas City May:3-13.

(11) Heady, E. O. and H. C. Madsen. 1973. National and
     interregional models of water demand for land use and
     agricultural policies, in G. G. Judge and T. Takayama,
     eds., Studies in Economic Planning Over Space and Time,
     North Holland Publishing Co., Amsterdam. (pps. 651-675)

(12) Holland, J. 1975. Input-output estimates of energy use
     in the Nebraska economy for 1967. unpublished M. A.
     thesis, University of Nebraska-Lincoln.

(13) Ireri, D. and H. O. Carter. 1970. California-Arizona economic interdependence and water transfer patterns, California Agricultural Experiment Station and Giannini Foundation of Agricultural Economics, Research Report 313, Berkeley.

(14) Lamphear, F. C. and T. W. Roesler. 1974. Impact analysis of irrigated agriculture on Nebraska's economy, 1967-1970. Nebraska Economic and Business Report Number 7, Bureau of Business Research, University of Nebraska-Lincoln.

(15) Lappala, E. G. undated. Impacts of drought on water utilization and storage. unpublished manuscript, U. S. Geological Survey, Lincoln.

(16) Lovett, J. V. (ed.) 1973. The Environmental, Economic and Social Significance of Drought, Angus and Robertson, Melbourne.

(17) Meadows, D. H., D. L. Meadows, J. Randers, and W. W. Behrens, III. 1972. The Limits to Growth, The New American Library, Inc., New York.

(18) Mesarovic, M. and E. Pestel. 1974. Mankind at the Turning Point, The New American Library, Inc., New York.

(19) Miernyk, W. H. 1975. Regional employment impacts of rising energy prices. Labor Law Journal 26:518-523.

(20) Miernyk, W. H. 1975. The regional economic consequences of high energy prices. Journal of Energy and Development 1:213-239.

(21) Richardson, H. W. 1972. Input-Output and Regional Economics, Halsted Press, John Wiley and Sons, New York.

(22) Riefler, R. F. 1973. Interregional input-output: a state of the arts survey, in G. G. Judge and T. Takayama, eds., Studies in Economic Planning Over Space and Time, North Holland Publishing Co, Amsterdam.

(23) Riefler, R. F. undated. Economic impact of prolonged drought on the state of Nebraska. unpublished manuscript, University of Nebraska-Lincoln.

(24) Romans, J. R. 1965. Capital Exports and Growth Among U. S. Regions, Wesleyan University Press, Middletown, Conn.

(25) The Lincoln Star, March 11, 1975. (p. 7)

(26) Warrick, R. A. 1975. Drought hazard in the United
      States: a research assessment. Monograph #NSF-RA-E-
      75-004, Institute of Behavioral Science, University of
      Colorado, Boulder, Col.

5

Social and Political Impacts of Drought

Robert D. Miewald

The designation of certain changes in an area's weather as "drought" is a social act. Drought is relative to some human standard. We are not concerned, after all, about the lack of precipitation in the Mojave. Perhaps we would not even care about moisture deficiencies in Kansas had we not been persuaded to stop thinking of that semi-arid territory as part of the Great American Desert. If we accept the conclusion of Skaggs (1) that "the one commonality of definitions of drought seems to be the arbitrariness," we are thrown back upon social perceptions as the source of effective knowledge about this event.

Despite the fact that drought is defined by the people who experience it, we know little about the interactions of humans and their environment during such an extreme condition. The common sense of it tells us that drought is bad but does not inform us about the dimensions of the calamity. Any number of estimates of the cost of the present drought are available and one can easily project doomsday scenarios about the impact of drought on an ailing economy. But we do not need pricetags to be able to say that it adds to the total amount of human misery. Having stated the obvious, however, we are faced with far more difficult questions involving how we experience drought and, more important, how a collective experience leads to demands for public action. We have not capitalized on the lessons of past droughts to the extent that there is a body of social science data which could aid makers of public policy. As Borchert (2) has shown, scholarly interest in drought is as cyclical as rainfall patterns in the Great Plains. If the rains come soon, this symposium may be the last word on the subject until 1995.

In Fiscal Year 1976, the federal government spent $290 million on research programs in the atmospheric sciences (3). Almost none of that work could be construed as having a direct bearing on social questions. That such a considerable expenditure did not result in any immediate practical benefit was indicated by the floundering of officials in the early months of 1977. Policy makers at all levels were forced to fall back on that weakest of political responses--the creation of "blue ribbon" commissions, study groups or task forces on drought. It would be unfair to disparage the hard work and real accomplishments of many of these groups, but certainly in some cases their creation was more important as symbolic action, as a gesture against the fact of human frailty in coping with nature's vagaries, and thus not too far removed from the rain dances of the Hopis.

We can no longer afford a spasmodic, piecemeal approach to the study of drought, nor can social science continue to be regarded as the junior partner in future research ventures. In another twenty years, even more circuits in an interdependent global society will have been completed. As was shown by the events of 1972-73 (droughts in Africa and the Soviet Union, adverse weather conditions in other food production centers, and the economic effects of the Arab oil embargo), drought can serve to intensify worldwide dislocations. The more organized we become, the more easily we can become disorganized if unprepared to deal with drought and other natural disasters.

A Research Agenda

The best one can do at the present is discuss in a systematic way what we do not know about the social and political impact of drought. Even that assignment, however, must be more than a call for more data about the interrelationship of man and nature. Numbers alone will not do the job, and any social scientist beginning work in this area has to come to grips with the enduring debates which still shake disciplines such as sociology and political science. The dispute centers on what are valid data in the social sciences and how those data in turn affect the behavior of the members of society (4). One might wish to avoid this, by now, tiresome argument, but its implications are particularly critical in the study of drought, based as it is on individual perceptions and not on absolute physical fact.

As an oversimplification, we can say that the empirical school holds that there is an objective social world which can be observed and measured by the scientist. Social reality is a basically stable object for inquiry and causal connections can be revealed. If x, then y; if drought, then a specific type of reaction. The social world differs in degree, but not in kind, from the physical world. The dissent-

ers to this view maintain, in essence, that social reality is
far more problematic. Reality is in a constant process of
redefinition and thus causal chains are elusive. The supposed impact of any event will generally be conditioned by
factors unsuspected by the outside observer.

An awareness of this divergence in approach is especially important in the study of natural events. On one extreme,
an earthquake probably does have a measurable impact on humans; there may well be a visceral reaction common to most
who experience the event so that the social world is merely
an extension of the physical. On the other extreme, drought
is characterized by a slow emergence, long duration and a
relative absence of dramatic incidents; it is primarily the
result of something (rainfall) not happening. In that case,
society has the opportunity to establish gradually a new re-
ciprocal relation with the natural environment. Drought is a
peculiarly social natural disaster and x does not always lead
to y. The network of mutual expectations which make up
social reality may change so unobtrusively that the natural
condition is not regarded as a crisis at all.

The study of drought, therefore, should focus on the relations between social and natural reality. What are the individual and collective responses to evidence that the world
is out of joint? In fact, is such evidence permitted to
emerge, or do people regard the drought, if perceived at all,
as an untoward event in an otherwise hospitable environment,
an event that will soon pass so life can return to normal?
To recommend that society adjust to the reality of the environment begs the question of what is perceived as reality.
We may now feel that those settlers who flocked to the Great
Plains because they believed that "rain follows the plow"
were suffering from a form of mass delusion. Yet today we
are unlikely to dismantle an extensive agricultural system
in that area to conform to the reality first described by
John Wesley Powell. According to a geographer (5), people
are "influenced quite as much by beliefs as by facts" about
their environment. While we might hope for a degree of con-
gruence between facts and beliefs, the creative function of
this type of cognitive dissonance cannot be overlooked.

As a framework upon which to hang the scanty evidence
available and with which to give structure to the many factors we do not know about drought, we shall start with a
social world in equilibrium, even if not in perfect harmony
with the natural world. That is, to everyone involved, the
world makes sense. By speculating on the disruptive effect
of drought in such a system, we can perhaps illuminate what
must be known and, in a positive manner, point out to policy

makers those gaps between social reality and a more intract-
able natural world. As a general introduction to an agenda
of needed research, it can be said that our knowledge is incomplete in each area of impact, from the individual to the
international level.

The Individual

The ancient Greeks, with their concern about the influence of "humors" on individual behavior, began a long tradition of theorizing about the effect of climate on society.
To be sure, there was a great deal of nonsense in these
theories (6). However, behavioral science might reconsider
its total abandonment of the tradition. Specifically, it
would be useful to have more information about the psycholog-
ical effect, if any, of prolonged drought. There are journalistic accounts of mental illness, crime and other deviant
behavior being stimulated by drought conditions, but not
much has been done in the way of scientific analysis. If
behavior does change with the weather, it would be necessary
to know if drought is a physiological influence or if personal deviance is instead caused by a perception of a dis-
tressing environment.

At a minimum, we need more work, along the line of the
pioneering research by Saarinen (7) on perceptions of drought
hazards, which will indicate probable individual reactions.
If drought is whatever the inhabitants of a region perceive
it to be, we must also know at what point the need for re-
medial action is felt. Heathcote (8) remarked on the tendency of rural Australians to "disregard" drought, which he
attributed to "a conscious, or unconscious, refusal to accept drought as a permanent characteristic of Australia..."
Brooks (9) expressed similar surprise at the ability of
peasants in northeastern Brazil to overlook the hazards of
drought. In effect, the question is when is drought no longer seen as "just one of those things" which an individual
must endure and instead is perceived as a social event requiring collective action. It is not a question which can
be answered by reading a rain gauge. Instead, what is needed is much more research on social variables in individual
cognition under extreme stress.

The Community

In face of adversity, what sort of support does the individual receive from family and friends? What compels one
to persevere rather than surrender to the elements? Conversely, since it is by no means certain that people will
always be kind, at what point does deprivation set neighbor

against neighbor and thus begin the disintegration of the community? Some answers might be found through an investigation of groups which have displayed considerable cohesion in surviving a drought. Writing of the survivors of a Nebraska drought that "exceeded all probability," Sandoz (10) claimed that "common need knit them closer." Another hypothesis worth testing holds that certain ethnic groups were better able than the more individualistic Yankees to adapt to harsh seasons. The same is true of religious communities such as the Mormons and Mennonites. During the 1976-77 drought, Nebraska Mennonites fed the cattle shipped to them by their co-religionists in affected areas in South Dakota (11). Such instances of private welfare may be insignificant compared to public programs, but further study might provide insights into the formation of social reality during hard times.

Of more than esthetic value would be a review of the culture of drought-prone areas and particularly of the "dust bowl" years on the Great Plains. Local culture--the art, literature, music and folklore of a region--especially under the most extreme conditions, can be taken as an expression by the victims that man shall prevail. Or, in the words of a folklorist (12), this culture is "a functional component of subsistence." As an "unessential artifact," culture implies that there is still hope; a dispirited community would not bother. What then was the essence of the cultural manifestations which could help to convince a people watching their livelihood blowing away that there was some purpose in staying on?

In general, the available information on community responses to drought has a distinctly rural flavor. Events of 1977 indicate the need for greater understanding of the effects of water shortages on an urban population. The perception of the drought hazard by city dwellers, as well as their subsequent adjustments, may be as crucial as that of the farmers. At what point, for example, can the urban water manager expect the citizens to respond to warnings of impending shortages? Just how effective are programs of voluntary conservation? What are the dynamics of rationing, and what are the political costs to the elected officials who must impose such restrictions? Most of our knowledge about urban drought is of a technical, waterworks-management nature, and in that area the technicians seem quite proficient (13). We need to supplement the technical knowledge with social science research on the effect of severe deprivation within that complex, heterogeneous entity which is the modern city. And, in an area related to our next topic, perhaps the most urgent research need involves the city's search for increased water

supplies. The right of eminent domain is a powerful weapon
with which thirsty municipalities can divert agricultural
water, thus disrupting the economic health of the rural hin-
terlands. Notions of "the public interest" are thrown about,
but little objective work has been done in defining that term
so that urban-rural conflict can be resolved for the benefit
of the largest number of citizens (14).

Inter-Community Relations

By the very nature of drought, a single community is a
limited unit for productive research. Put another way, a
drought raises serious questions about what, in a political
sense, is a community. Most studies of water policy support
the contention of Ingram (15) that "wherever water is situat-
ed, it is locally thought of as 'our' water." But as Warwick notes, the social consequences of water shortages, and
particularly of drought, are expanding in geographical scope
(16). In a federal system such as ours, the existence of
several thousand independent units of government sets the
stage for considerable conflict over a scarce resource. Are
we then more likely to see increased intergovernmental conflict or greater cooperation as a response to drought?

The Western Region Drought Action Task Force (17) found
that the combined efforts against the 1977 drought "has
reflected intergovernmental cooperation at its best." A
casual observer, however, might be more impressed with signs
of tension within the federal structure. If all the threatened lawsuits between governments come to trial, the courts
will face crowded dockets for a long time. The verbal duels
of governors over weather modification proposals (or "cloud
stealing" according to downwind states) provide other examples. In California, the drought has revived all the latent animosities between North and South (18). However, a
California appeals court has recently put forth a rather bold
definition of the community. In a memorandum to the latest
case involving the long-standing water disputes of Los Angeles
and the Owens Valley (19), the court found that "when the
state's water resources dwindle, the constitutional demands
grow more stringent and compelling, to the end that scarcity
and personal sacrifice be distributed as widely as possible
among the state's inhabitants." Such an assertion that
"we're all in this together" may be easier to make than to
implement.

While admitting that the current drought has "provided
many examples of how the federal system of government can
function with local, state and national units working coop-
eratively and in concert to provide an essential service to

the people," a California water expert (20) noted several
strains in federal-state relations as well as "in the relationships of state and local agencies, and between water dis-
tributors and their customers." The matter should be regarded as an exciting opportunity for students of intergovernmental relations. Many of the models of federalism have been
put to a severe test by drought.

In particular, the provocative theories of Vincent Ostrom need reexamination in light of the recent drought. His
thesis, stated most fully in his report to the National Water
Commission, is that water policy is dominated by a "water industry," composed of both public and private institutions
(21). This industry is motivated to achieve high productivity through market mechanisms and the entrepreneurship of the
water managers. The system, which Ostrom advises against
modifying, may not function as smoothly as hoped when, as in a
drought, citizens are stimulated to pay more attention to the
distribution of water. The Lake Mission Viejo case (a recreational lake in Orange County was filled while Marin County
was under tight water rationing) might be reasonable from
Ostrom's "public choice" perspective; Bay Area Californians
regarded it as an outrage (22). A similar case has arisen in
the Pacific Northwest where residents watch hydroelectricity
exported from their power-short region in order to meet the
contractual obligations of the managers. The "water industry" model might make sense in times of surplus or even of
moderate shortage, but does it really provide for political
accountability under drought conditions? Conversely, as the
public choice theorist might respond, if we are truly inter-
ested in the most efficient use of water, can all the deli-
cate arrangements be subjected to control by an overly emo-
tional public? Drought-induced scarcity makes clear that
there are a number of unresolved issues in the area of intergovernmental relations.

Regional Impact

By regional, we refer to the social and economic structures of an extended geographical area and the interface of
these structures with the rest of the nation. We will discuss below the regional adaptations made possible through
subsidies from outside, both direct (relief efforts) and indirect (public works for water augmentation). Migration--
the most common form of adaptation throughout history--will
be examined here. Through the 1930s, migration was also the
traditional American response to drought. Although the likelihood of major migration has apparently decreased, we should
reconsider the nature of past migrations. For example, it
may be that past droughts only hastened the decision to move

on the part of more transient farmers. Also, drought may
have been a convenient excuse for moving; Stein (23) argues
that the refugees from the dust bowl preferred to believe
they had been defeated by impersonal nature rather than by
human actors. The last two major droughts (1950s and 1970s)
were not characterized by migration, but we still need more
information about those individual decisions which might
trigger a large-scale exodus from the drought area. The survey by Ottoson and his colleagues of Nebraska farmers during
the 1956 drought was useful in revealing the variables sepa-
rating those who remained from those who sold out (24). Such
work should be updated.

Of course, an easy assumption is that population decline
is proof of a healthy adjustment to the environment. The
population, after adjustment, will be more in line with what
the natural resources system can reasonably support. But
while the nomads may be able to fold their tents and as si-
lently steal away, a modern society is far more complex. The
emigrants leave behind an elaborate and often expensive institutional structure--schools, churches, commercial interests, local governments--which may then be unable to support
themselves, thus leading to inferior services at greater cost
for those remaining. Until we have more evidence, we must
assume that the supposed adjustment can cause as many problems for state and local governments as it solves.

Even if drought is no longer a cause of mass migration,
it still must be considered within the larger context of
national demographics. As the nation moves toward the establishment of an "urban growth policy" which aims at the prevention of dense concentrations of people in a few unmanage-
able urban centers, it is all the more urgent to be aware of
those special cases driving population from rural areas into
the cities. Indeed, even in the absence of a formal policy,
nonmetropolitan population seems to have stabilized (25). If
this is a good thing (and most commentators feel it is), we
should recognize that events such as drought can undermine an
emerging stability. Another factor worthy of consideration
is that, in general, normal migration is into rather than out
of potential drought areas. The movement of population from
the more humid North into the "sun belt" states such as Arizona and California means that more people are settling in
the areas most susceptible to drought.

A final aspect of regional adjustment to drought through
migration is its superficial appearance as a grand solution.
That is, the truism that there is an optimal number of people
who can support themselves in any area finds its way into the
policy process as a great profundity. The concept of "carry-

ing capacity" has become a part of modern political rhetoric and, in fact, the term has been recommended as a moral imperative (26). But if public officials consider suggestions for limiting population in areas subject to natural hazards (drought, floods, hurricanes, etc.) in relation to other proposals to encourage migration from areas of chronic unemployment, energy shortages or sheer population density, there is surely an obligation to answer one major question: Where is this paradise to which the "excess" population is expected to retire? If such a place exists, the local officials are probably about to follow the lead of Petaluma, California and Boulder, Colorado in passing "no-growth" legislation (27). The matter of population movement requires the most careful investigation, especially in view of the Carter administration's apparent intention of incorporating so-called "non-structural solutions" within a national water policy (28).

The Public Sphere

How does drought become a public issue? One intriguing line of research has been ignored since it was first suggested over fifty years ago (29). Drought seems to be related to extraordinary electoral behavior in the affected areas. The party preferences of American voters are fairly stable, but in some states there are occasional deviations from one-party domination. These deviations sometimes seem associated with drought patterns. In Nebraska, for example, elections since the turn of the century show a surge in minority party strength in 1908-10, 1934-38, 1948, 1958 and 1976. Excluding 1948, the state suffered from drought before or during the campaigns. Much more research on these apparent relationships is needed before even a tentative conclusion could be offered, but the results might be significant.

The significance of such electoral deviations would lie in the evidence they provide for a measure of political instability. The voters obviously are not anticipating that the new public officials will make it rain. The polls are a convenient place to express, in a socially acceptable manner, one's sense of frustration with weather conditions. A primary question is whether such frustration may be further expressed in more disruptive ways such as participation in extremist political movements. The Midwest, noted for its conservatism, is also well-known for political insurgency and the "political prairie fires" which have swept through the area. Some of these movements seem to have been stimulated, in part, by unfavorable growing conditions (30). More analysis of agrarian radicalism would be valuable in the development of a theory of political instability under future drought conditions.

But too much can be made of instability and partisan-
ship. The experience of the past forty years reveals little
difference between the Democratic and Republican approach to
short-term public policy about drought. There is virtually
no disagreement about the propriety of government providing
emergency relief for the victims of drought.

Much research remains to be done on the operation of
drought relief programs. It is difficult even to determine
their cost. Of course, part of the problem is that drought-
related expenses are often inseparable from ordinary government programs. For example, those put out of work by drought
cannot be identified when they collect unemployment benefits.
But for the programs aimed specifically at drought relief, we
still have to be satisfied with very incomplete data. The
Link study is the definitive work for the 1930s drought (31).
Her data are limited to the eight states most affected by the
drought and thus give an inaccurate picture of the national
drought program. Even so, all programs in the years from
1933 through 1936 could not have cost the federal government
more than a billion dollars. The data for the 1950s are no
less confusing, but whether one uses Congressional or Presidential figures, it seems unlikely that more than a billion
dollars were directly chargeable to drought relief over a
three-year period (32).

Even taking into account that we are using unadjusted
dollars, it seems clear that the cost of drought has increased in the 1970s. In the ten-month period ending March
31, 1977, the Federal Disaster Assistance Administration had
expended $46,101,078 in direct emergency relief (33). This
was before the major drought legislation of the 95th Congress
(P.L. 95-18 and P.L. 95-31) went into effect. During the
first three months of the new legislation, nearly $800 mil-
lion had been obligated (34). More impressive are the press
service reports of September 1, 1977 that nearly $8 billion
in long-term (30-40 years) loans had been committed. A single year of drought, in short, has diverted a large sum of
federal money from other uses.

Whatever the final figures for the current drought turn
out to be, numbers alone will not tell us if the total cost
represents a sufficient response by government. Emergency
relief is necessarily exempt from the analysis of the regular
budgetary process. When people are in a desperate situation,
the American political system responds quickly in meeting the
most urgent needs. Or so it appears on the surface. It is
not inhumane to suggest that these programs should be the object of the most intensive post-crisis scrutiny. First of
all, we need some idea whether the measures used were in fact

the most efficient ways of providing immediate relief for the
problems caused by drought. This sort of analysis would provide a basis for drafting proposals for future contingencies.
The uncertain response, in early 1977, of the Carter administration to Congressional initiatives in drought legislation
illustrates that the public and its politicians are not satisfied by pleas for further study once the crisis is upon us
(35).

Beyond the matter of program effectiveness, we must be
prepared at some future date to consider calmly the long-term
policy implications of relief programs. Unfortunately, disaster relief of any kind in the United States is a strange
combination of humanitarian impulses and political machina-
tions, all within an unwieldy administrative structure, so
that accurate evaluation of the end results of the policy is
seldom even attempted. What is obvious is that disaster relief is becoming an increasingly expensive proposition and,
at a time when we are finally aware that we can afford only
so many government programs, we should be ready at least to
consider less costly alternatives. And since we have paid
little attention to the side effects of drought relief, one
must agree with Warwick (36) that "a closer examination of
the more long-term system effects is warranted."

A greater appreciation of the effect of emergency relief
would be essential if and when officials begin the development of a long-range policy toward the drought threat. To be
sure, there have been a number of adjustments to the drought
problem over the years, but it is doubtful whether these adjustments have been the result of a conscious government policy. Attempts at developing such a policy have been unsuccessful. Hargreaves concludes that the interest in land-use
planning, stimulated by the 1930s drought, soon faded (37).
The hope of President Eisenhower (38), expressed during the
drought of the 1950s, that government was finally about to
take seriously the need for "long-range solutions that will
help keep future drought from being future disasters" was
unjustified, since that period did not see the creation of a
coherent policy on drought. Whether the Carter administration will have more success in making drought a prime consideration in its new national water policy remains to be seen.
Carter's first months in office support the notion that he is
committed to the idea that " 'wise management and conservation' may be better answers to water problems than the expensive construction projects of the past" (39). Such a change
in direction might make the nation better able to husband its
water resources in good times and bad, but it is far too
early to tell whether the President can convince Congress and
the public.

Finally, in terms of a public policy toward drought, it
must be recognized that we have tended to focus our attention
too much on the federal government. We need a more complete
knowledge of the alternatives open to those at the state and
local level who will feel the first demands for government
action. Many states and localities have had long experience
with governmental actions designed to counter the impact of
drought. Typical actions in the past have included state aid
to drought-stricken areas, the enactment of special social
security legislation, the imposition of new taxes (such as
liquor and gasoline surcharges) in order to provide funds for
emergency relief, moratoria on loans and foreclosures, diversion of state highway contracts to affected regions, and the
promotion of private relief efforts. Little is known about
these programs since they are soon forgotten after the
drought. Certainly it is to be hoped that the work of the
several state drought task forces will be documented so that
their successors in the next drought will not have to start
from point zero. In short, a detailed inventory of drought
programs and their effectiveness would be of great help to
public officials.

International Relations

The impact of a sustained drought in the major grain-
producing areas of the United States would be felt throughout the rest of the world. The news that American agriculture is presently suffering from a massive surplus of basic
foodstuffs should not make us ignore the critical fact that
world food production rates still lag behind population increase. Because of the growing dependence of other countries
on American commodities, future droughts may cause more serious problems than in previous years. The global impact of
the 1972 crop failure in the Soviet Union suggests the kind
of effect on the world economy which might be anticipated.

The term "politics of food" has been used widely in recent years, but the direction this new brand of politics is
to take is not completely clear. A major source of confusion
is the divergence of goals of American foreign policy. One
implication is that our food-producing capacity should be a
major weapon of foreign policy, a counterweight to the resource cartels in the conduct of "economic warfare" (40).
If such a policy is to be pursued, the national interest demands that there be a more effective coordination of farm and
foreign policy to insure that the granary (or arsenal) is
never empty.

We have tended to believe that the American national interest is best served by maintaining stability throughout the

world. Famine, especially in the developing countries, is a
major source of instability. The architecture of stability,
however, may come into conflict with our traditional humanitarianism which holds that mass starvation is an ameliorable
evil in itself. A drought which reduces American food reserves may place before policy makers some awful alternatives.
But to what extent can any foreign politics of food be expected to succeed in face of demands from American producers
and consumers? In the words of one authority (41), "Experience demonstrates that willingness to supply food is much influenced by the availability of food that can be exported
without increasing domestic prices or forcing consummers to
to turn to less preferred, if still nutritional, diets." As
the unedifying debates over embargoes in the 1976 campaign
illustrated, some serious thought should be devoted to priorities before it is too late for anything other than a spasm
response to natural events.

Whether the impulse to alleviate famine is motivated by
humanitarianism or by more instrumental reasons, American
decision makers might profit from a review of our political
and administrative capabilities and limitations as evidenced
by past emergencies. The response to famine in the drought-
stricken regions of Sahelian Africa was marked by many mis-
takes which should not be repeated (42). Whether the prompt
provision of emergency relief was prevented by the inertia
of our own agencies, the balky nature of multinational organizations, or the corruption of native governments is not
the point. Instead, there are lessons to be derived from
that rather unhappy exercise which need not be relearned during the next life-and-death struggle with famine.

On Institutional Arrangements

The foregoing is not a complete list of research needs;
rather, it is intended to show that a literature on the social and political impact of drought is virtually nonexistent.
There are, however, two features that deserve further attention. These are the administrative and political systems.
When addressing environmental problems, natural scientists
have a tendency to call for "improved institutional arrangements" in order that better use be made of their growing
understanding of the physical world. There is a danger that
a term like "institutional arrangements" will make social and
political adjustment sound too easy, as if institutions can
in fact be rearranged on demand or that the new arrangements
will perform as expected. It is the resistant nature of
these very institutions which perpetuates the incongruence
between natural and social reality.

Institutions are not something outside of social reality, to be manipulated at will by masterful engineers. Instead, they are very much the concrete manifestation of our social reality. History is full of examples of institutions which tried to impose an artificial reality upon a stubborn nature. In the past, such heroic attempts were generally overwhelmed by the facts and, in effect, society had to accept the truth of a new reality. Modern organizations, however, are better prepared to beat down the environment, at least in the short run, through technological marvels. In terms of drought, if our institutions encourage us to continue to regard it as just another temporary disturbance in an otherwise stable world, a new reality will not be able to emerge. The problem will be "solved" only in the sense that a great deal of energy and money will be spent until normal rainfall patterns return. But society may not have moved toward an adjustment to the fact of drought.

Administration

Public institutions charged with the responsibility of administering a response to drought will obviously have to be improved. But how? Administration is nothing more than a supposedly coherent series of rational decisions. A rational decision in turn demands a fairly reliable body of knowledge about an organization's environment. Organizations do not aspire to complete rationality, but instead are usually content to know "just enough" about the environments they are charged with modifying (43). When we consider the record of agencies, such as the post office, whose environments are relatively stable and precisely mapped, how bleak seem the prospects for an efficient administration of public solutions to drought.

The immediate problem is the simple lack of knowledge. Without that solid base, administrative dysfunctions are to be expected. White and Haas (44) argue that, in the absence of complete knowledge, public agencies in disasters "turn to readily available technological solutions..." Specifically, they suggest that the Bureau of Reclamation has favored cloud seeding over research into water consumption and land-use management. However, recent testimony concerning proposed federal support for cloud seeding operations indicates that administrators can also use the lack of information to justify a rather complacent course of action in the face of an emergency; rather than take chances with weather modification techniques, the administrators argued for further study. And in the meantime, as one Congressman replied, the farmers would have to go back to plowing their six inches of dust (45).

Although Bhattacharya (46) maintains that drought is precisely the sort of emergency that can jar administration out of its bounded rationality and bureaucratic routines, it is unrealistic to recommend that we simply hope things will work out well in a crisis. Even after the knowledge base is expanded, it is likely that the administrative action will be less than effective, primarily because the nature of drought does not provide the clues needed for an immediate response. As the American Red Cross (47) noted of the drought of 1930, "There was nothing spectacular about the drought. There was no one dramatic day, with its terror and anguish and supreme tests of courage." The lack of unambiguous signals was at the root of Senator George McGovern's (48) criticism about the administrative response to "intermediate type disasters which are regional in scope and which continue over a protracted period of time." The comment of an American official (49) about the reactions of African governments to the Sahelian drought--"It sneaked up on them over a five-year period"--could probably apply as well to more advanced administrative systems.

If administrative relief for drought is not to fall as unevenly and unfairly as the rain, and if the nation is not to be bankrupted by extravagant programs, we will need to develop far more sensitivity to a variety of conditions than we are accustomed to expect from public administration. There will be no perfect solution here, even when the technical state of the art of drought management is improved by further research. Administration, with its budgetary constraints and abstract categories, is necessarily the embodiment of an impoverished view of reality. Administration is bound to the past from whence it derived its knowledge. Even with that major limitation, however, some marginal improvements can be attempted. A top research priority must be the investigation of the responses of the resource manager to drought. We need more work like that of Russell, Arey and Kates (50) on the manager's perception of the beginning, duration and end of drought conditions. Such studies, together with case studies of administrative behavior during the current drought, could at least help us to estimate the limits of the possible in drought administration.

The Political Process

According to our political theory, administrative deficiencies, including the tendency of bureaucrats to administer a world which no longer exists, are to be corrected by a democratic political overhead. To what extent are our political institutions effective in framing a wise public response to drought? And if they are ineffective, what changes must be

made in our way of conducting public business so that we are
in harmony with the natural world? These questions are being
asked more often as we move from an era of abundance into an
era of scarcity.

The matter is all the more urgent in water resources
management. Even in years of normal precipitation, the old
ways of allocation are showing strain under the pressure of
increased demand. Mann (51) notes that, in terms of the cat-
gories used by students of public policy, water policy is
undergoing a drastic change which will shake the foundations
of water management institutions. The traditional approach
has been "distributive;" that is, local units have been able
to support a variety of uncoordinated projects, of limited
and sometimes dubious value, by tapping a general source of
public wealth. Distributive politics have been wasteful, and
by virtue of that prodigality, we have avoided a number of
unpleasant choices. The new emphasis on ecology and the
perception of a scarcity of resources underscores Mann's assertion that "distributive politics defies even an approach
to rationality. It disguises or masks the systemic consequences while relying on the total system through the trea-
sury to provide benefits to the local interests involved."
But it is doubtful whether the added burden of drought will
lead to a different style in water policy making.

An Illustrative Case

Because water is regarded as an American's birthright,
according to the National Academy of Sciences (52), "in the
public allocation process it is unlikely that society will
welcome widespread and strict allocation of water." It does
not seem that a widely publicized drought in the 1970s has
changed this central feature of our social reality. President Carter's unsuccessful frontal assault on the water policy sub-system is one indication of the endurance of the old
political patterns. But if change is to come, perhaps the
first signs will be at the local level, in those small units
which are at the core of the distributive mode.

Events in Nebraska illustrate that institutional reform
alone is not enough to alter significantly our basic approach
to water shortages. Through the creation, in 1972, of multi-
purpose resource management districts (Natural Resources Districts), that state has gone as far as one could expect in
the improvement of the institutional arrangements. Had they
been created in an earlier decade, the NRDs might have experienced a serene existence by performing for their predomi-
nantly rural constituents a range of essential services of a
distributive nature. However, they have been thrust into the

center of the controversy over the need for the regulation of
the state's most precious resource--its groundwater supply.
In 1975, the legislature passed the sensitive issue on to the
NRDs through passage of a groundwater control act. The act
empowers the districts to institute restrictions on well irrigation in areas of critically low reserves.

Despite three consecutive dry growing seasons and an
even longer period of discussion of groundwater problems, it
was not until July, 1977 that the first concrete steps were
taken by an NRD to impose groundwater controls. Still to be
resolved are the specific control measures, and it can be assumed that NRDs and irrigators will have trouble in agreeing
upon the type of regulation to be imposed, especially since
no consensus exists among Nebraska farmers that the control
of groundwater is a proper function of any government.

The interesting point is that NRDs, as truly modernized
institutions, are acting like any other unit of government
when faced with irreconcilable conflict; they are looking for
the technological solution. If there is not enough water to
go around, resolve the issue not be allotting that which is
available but instead by "creating" more. Now the districts
appear to be intrigued by the possibility of transbasin diversion. Although their plans are more limited than those of
other states which would reroute the Yukon or Mississippi,
Nebraskans seem about to seek legal permission to move around
large quantities of water within the state. This sort of
public works project will involve considerable amounts of
money, and it is uncertain if urban interests will be as ac-
quiescent as in the past in supporting them. Already the
diversion projects have captured the attention of other users
of water; they are afraid "their" water will not be available
when needed. In short, there is just not enough water to
meet all needs, and no juggling can hide the fact.

The ultimate responsibility for water distribution re-
sides with the legislature, but that body does not appear
eager to provide guidance. In the session of 1977, when public concern with drought seems to have been at a peak, the
state senators deliberately avoided the reconsideration of
the state's water laws. The need for further study was given
as the reason for delay. If that was the real reason (and
not reluctance to participate in a zero-sum game), the action
illustrates a basic problem in responding to drought: Is it
better to act in haste while the public is most concerned, or
to approach the issue cautiously and thus risk losing widespread public support after the crisis has passed? Since the
rains appear to have returned to Nebraska, the next session
of the legislature should provide some answers.

As of this writing, the drought of the 1970s does not seem to have had a significant impact on the way in which Nebraskans regard the issue of water. We would need, however, case studies from other states before more definite conclusions about the effect of drought on our style of politics are possible. If past droughts are any guide, it may be expected that there has not been a dramatic change in our basic expectations about water allocation. And if we put our faith in changing only the institutions and not the underlying political attitudes, we will be unable to cope with further scarcity. Institutions simply cannot be arranged so that we can all be supported in the manner to which we have become accustomed. And allocative patterns will not be easier to change under a crisis caused by drought.

Conclusion

Drought has the potential for causing profound shocks to our political and economic systems, despite the most valiant attempts to maintain the status quo. In the 1930s, of course, we were resilient enough to overcome the combined impact of prolonged drought and economic depression. The troublesome question is whether we have retained our resiliency. Or is it possible that we are overly dependent upon "normal" weather and thus cannot adjust to the inevitable deviations from normality? We had a dramatic and very disquieting foretaste of some frightening possibilities in the summer of 1977. One hundred years ago, a thunderstorm was a local inconvenience; today, if we are to believe Con Ed, it is enough to immobilize our largest city, disrupt national communications and, worst of all, cause a drastic collapse of social cohesion.

If we learn nothing from the current drought, then it may be said that the worst impact is no real impact at all. If we are arrogant enough to belive we have solved a problem just because it begins to rain, then our shared social reality will not have been affected. That would mean a return to business as usual, a return to dependence upon a quite undependable "normality." It would mean a return to regarding water as a free and unlimited resource. Water use could then be pushed to even more unrealistic limits, and the recurrence of drought will be all the more painful.

But one final caution is due here. At least since biblical times, drought has brought out the best (or worst) in prophets of doom. If we are responsible for the creation of a social reality which does not recognize the severe limitations of nature, we still should not be hasty in making the social world a mere extension of the natural. Scholarship would serve us poorly if the idea of limits is reified, that

condition, according to Berger and Luckmann (53), "whereby
the objectivated world loses its comprehensibility as a human
enterprise and becomes fixated as a non-human, non-
humanizable, inert facticity." Further research might have
such a deadening effect if it results only in what Lofland
(54) describes as "bigger, larger and stronger statistical
statements" which can "embody an imagery of domination, of
overwhelming existence, and of an iron fatefulness in how
social variations are hooked together..." More simply put,
even though a new social reality about the use of natural
resources may be desirable, it must be remembered that much
of human progress can be understood as a stubborn defiance of
reality. Long-forgotten guardians of reality, after all,
once assured us that the world was flat and that man could
not fly. It is to be hoped, in other words, that increased
knowledge about drought does not lead to a passive fatalism,
but instead is the basis of a more effective challenge of the
environment.

References

(1) Skaggs, R. 1975. Drought in the United States, 1931-
     40. Annals of the Association of American Geographers.
     65:391-402.

(2) Borchert, J.R. 1971. The dust bowl in the 1970s. An-
     nals of the Association of American Geographers. 61:1-
     22.

(3) Federal Council for Science and Technology. 1975. Nat-
     ional Atmospheric Sciences Program: Fiscal Year 1976.
     Washington, GPO.

(4) Bernstein, R.J. 1976. The Restructuring of Social and
     Political Theory. New York, Harcourt, Brace Jovanovich.

(5) Brown, R.H. 1948. Historical Geography of the United
     States. New York, Harcourt, Brace and World.

(6) Thomas, F. 1925. The Environmental Basis of Society.
     New York, Century.

(7) Saarinen, T.F. 1966. Perceptions of the Drought Hazard
     on the Great Plains. Dept. of Geography, University of
     Chicago, Res. Paper No. 106.

(8) Heathcote, R.L. 1973. Drought perception. In J.V. Lo-
     vett, ed., The Environmental, Economic and Social Signi-
     ficance of Drought. Sydney, Angus and Robertson.

(9) Brooks, R.H. 1975. Drought and public policy in north-
     eastern Brazil. Ekistics. 39:30-35.

(10) Sandoz, M. 1935. Old Jules. New York, Hastings House.

(11) Conversation with H. Troyer, pastor of the Mennonite
     Church, Milford, Nebraska, 13 September 1977.

(12) Welsch, R. 1972. Shingling the Fog and Other Plains
     Lies. Chicago, Swallow.

(13) May, 1977. Rationing ends cheap water myth. The Amer-
     ican City and County. 92:66-68.

(14) Radosevich, G.E. and M.B. Sabey. 1977. Water rights,
     eminent domain, and the public interest. Water Re-
     sources Bull. 13:747-757.

(15) Ingram, H. 1969. Patterns of Politics in Water Re-
     sources Development. Albuquerque, University of New
     Mexico, Div. of Govt. Res., Pub. No. 79.

(16) Warwick, R. 1975. Drought Hazard in the United States.
     Boulder, University of Colorado, Inst. of Behavioral
     Science.

(17) Western Region Drought Action Task Force. 1977. Di-
     rectory of Federal Drought Assistance 1977. Washington,
     Dept. of Agriculture.

(18) Los Angeles Times. Feb. 10, 1977. Dry north looks
     south, sees red.

(19) Cited in: Los Angeles Times. April 3, 1977. Water
     sharing: We reach a milestone. The case is County of
     Inyo v. City of Los Angeles, App., 139 Cal. Rptr. 396.

(20) Warne, W.E. July, 1977. New problems arise from the
     Western drought. ASPA News and Views, 27:1, 17-19.

(21) Ostrom, V. 1971. Institutional Arrangements for Water
     Resources Development. National Water Commission, Ar-
     lington, Va.

(22) Los Angeles Times. Feb. 6, 1977. California contrast:
     Drought and a new lake.

(23) Stein, W. 1973. California and the Dust Bowl Migra-
     tion. Westport, Greenwood Press.

(24) Ottoson, H.W., et.al. 1966. Land and People in the Northern Plains Transition Area. Lincoln, U. of Neb. Press.

(25) Fuguitt, G.V. 1971. The places left behind: Population trends and policy for rural America. Rural Sociology. 36:449-470.

(26) Hardin, G. 1976. Carrying capacity as an ethical concept. Soundings. 59:121-137.

(27) Morrison, P.A. 1977. Migration and Rights of Access: New Public Concerns of the 1970s. Santa Monica, Rand Paper P-5785.

(28) Kirschten, J.D. 1977. Draining the water projects out of the pork barrel. National Journal. 9:540-548.

(29) Barnhart, J.D. 1925. Rainfall and the populist party in Nebraska. Am. Pol. Sci. Rev. 19:527-540.

(30) Shover, J.L. 1965. Cornbelt Rebellion. Urbana, University of Illinois Press.

(31) Link, I. 1937. Relief and Rehabilitation in the Drought Area. Works Progress Admin., Div. of Soc. Res. Bull. Ser. 5, No. 3, Washington, GPO.

(32) U.S. House of Representatives. 1957. Drought Relief Program. Hearings before the Committee on Agriculture, Ser. B. Washington, GPO; Special Assistant to the President for Public Works Planning, 1958. Drouth: A Report. Washington, GPO.

(33) U.S. Senate. 1977. Community Emergency Drought Relief Act of 1977. Hearings before the Committee on Environment and Public Works. Washington, GPO.

(34) New York Times. July 31, 1977. Cost of emergency relief soars for "worst drought in century."

(35) U.S. Senate. 1977. Drought Authority. Hearings before the Committee on Energy and Natural Resources. Washington, GPO.

(36) Warwick, op. cit.

(37) Hargreaves, M. 1976. Land-use planning in response to drought: The experience of the thirties. Agricultural History. 50:561-582.

(38) President of the United States. 1957. Alleviating Emergency Conditions Brought about by Prolonged Drought and Other Severe Natural Disasters, House Doc. No. 110. Washington, GPO.

(39) Kirschten, J.D. 1977. Turning back the tides of long-time federal water policy. National Journal. 9:900-903.

(40) Schneider, W. 1976. Food, Foreign Policy, and Raw Materials Cartels. New York, Crane, Russak.

(41) Brandow, G.E. 1977. The place of U.S. food in eliminating world hunger. Annals of the American Acad. of Pol. and Soc. Sciences. 429:8-16.

(42) Sheets, H. and R. Morris. 1974. Disaster in the Desert: Failures of International Relief in the West African Drought. Washington, Carnegie Endowment for International Peace.

(43) Miewald, R.D. 1978. Public Administration: A Critical Perspective. New York, McGraw-Hill.

(44) White, G.F. and J.E. Haas. 1975. Assessment of Research on Natural Hazards. Cambridge, M.I.T. Press.

(45) U.S. House of Representatives. 1976. Drought Emergency Relief Act of 1976. Hearings before the Committee on Agriculture. Washington, GPO.

(46) Bhattacharya, M. 1975. Emergency administration: A study of drought-relief operations in an Indian state. J. of Administration Overseas. 14:259-265.

(47) American Red Cross. 1931. Relief Work in the Drought of 1930-31. Washington, American Red Cross.

(48) U.S. Senate. 1976. Disaster Program Evaluation. Hearings before the Committee on Agriculture and Forestry. Washington, GPO.

(49) Glantz, M.H. (ed.). 1976. The Politics of Natural Disaster: The Case of the Sahel Drought. New York, Praeger.

(50) Russell, C.S., D.G. Arey and R.W. Kates. 1970. Drought and Water Supply. Baltimore, Johns Hopkins.

(51) Mann, D.E. 1975. Political incentives in U.S. water policy: Relationships between distributive and regula-

tory politics.   In M. Holden and D. L. Dresang, eds.,
What Government Does.   Beverly Hills, Sage.

(52) National Academy of Sciences.   1966.   Alternatives in
Water Management.   Washington, Nat. Acad. of Sciences.

(53) Berger, P.L. and T. Luckmann.   1967.   The Social Construction of Reality.   New York, Anchor Books.

(54) Lofland, J.   1976.   Doing Social Life: The Qualitative
Study of Human Interactions in Natural Settings.   New
York, John Wiley.

6

Strategies in the
Event of Drought

J. Eugene Haas

      Periodic drought is one of more than a dozen significant geophysical hazards faced by Americans, (White and Haas, 1975). Figure 1 indicates that drought is second only to flood and frost in direct loss produced annually. Unlike most geophysical hazards which have a relatively quick onset and short duration, drought is a creeping phenomenon. Significant losses to drought can occur in almost any area of the country.

      An overview of the social consequences of drought may be seen in Figure 2.

Adjustments to Drought: Agriculture

      Adjustments to drought in agricultural enterprises differ in part from those for urban areas, and therefore they will be discussed separately. An adjustment is any adaptation intended to preclude, decrease or cope with anticipated or actual losses from a geophysical hazard. Figure 3 represents a range of adjustments to drought which have been utilized to various degrees in the United States since 1930.

      From an analytical perspective there are two basic approaches which can be used in trying to cope with the drought hazard: modification of aspects of the geophysical events *per se* and modification of some part(s) of the agricultural enterprise. See Table 1.

      It is useful to view as one large *system* the complex set of geophysical processes and linkages combined with agricultural practices and investments. Thus, we may speak of a *natural* event *subsystem* and an *agricultural subsystem* (Warrick, 1975).

      The natural event subsystem is composed of meteorologi-

FIGURE 1

MEAN ANNUAL LOSSES

HAZARD	DEATHS per 10 Million	INJURIES per 10 Million	PROPERTY DAMAGE 1▭6 $ PER CAPITA
Avalanche	.35	.48	▪
Coastal Erosion	–	–	▬
Drought	–	–	▬▬▬
Earthquake	.38	?	▪
Flood	3.90	?	▬▬▬▬
Frost	–	–	▬▬▬▬
Hail	–	–	▬▬
Hurricane	2.52	119.52	▬▬
Landslide	–	–	▪
Lightning	5.43	10.95	▪
Tornado	5.24	90.48	▬▬
Tsunami	1.57	?	'
Urban Snow	5.19	3.19	'
Volcano	NA	NA	NA
Windstorm	4.65	29.42	▬

NA – Not Applicable

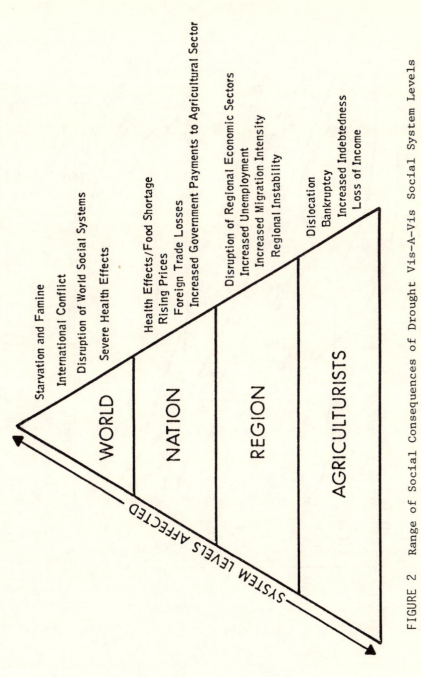

FIGURE 2   Range of Social Consequences of Drought Vis-A-Vis Social System Levels

FIGURE 3   Generalized Historical Trends of Drought Adjustment

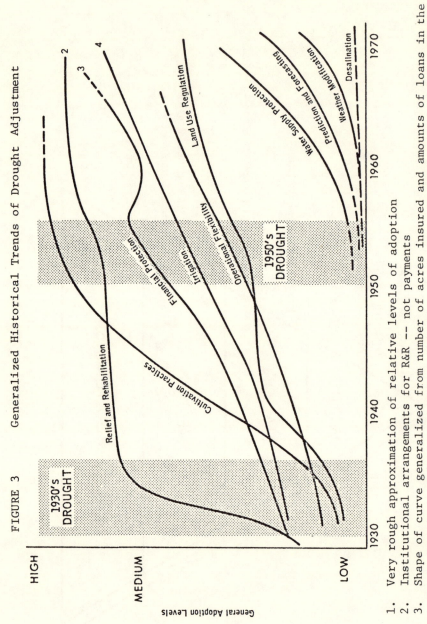

1. Very rough approximation of relative levels of adoption
2. Institutional arrangements for R&R -- not payments
3. Shape of curve generalized from number of acres insured and amounts of loans in the
   United States (dip in 1950's reflects lower adoption of insurance at that time)
4. Based on total irrigated acres in the United States

TABLE 1

ADJUSTMENTS TO DROUGHT: AGRICULTURE

I. MODIFICATION OF NATURAL EVENT SUBSYSTEM

 A. Augmentation of Water

 Modification of precipitation
 Use of irrigation

 B. Conservation of Water

 Cultivation practices

 Water supply protection

II. MODIFICATION OF AGRICULTURAL SUBSYSTEM

 A. Alter Agricultural Characteristics

 Operational flexibility

 Land use management

 Prediction and forecasting

 B. Spread/Share Losses and Costs

 Financial protection

 Relief and rehabilitation

cal and hydrological elements. As will be seen, some aspects
of each component can be altered in attempting to adjust to
the drought hazard.

Modification of the Natural Event Subsystem.

Here possible modifications in meteorological and
hydrological components are considered.

A. Augmentation of Water. For several decades there
have been efforts to increase precipitation by "seeding"
clouds with chemicals, especially silver iodide. The concept
is that mother nature is sometimes quite inefficient and,
therefore only a fraction of the available moisture in the
atmosphere over a given area falls out as precipitation. The
insertion of silver iodide provides a greatly increased number of condensation nuclei around which droplets may form,
thus making the precipitation process more efficient. It is
fair to say, however, that at best there is only a modest
beginning of an adequate understanding of the physical processes involved in attempting to increase precipitation
(Hess, 1974).

Some field experimental work has been conducted on precipitation augmentation. By far the most common practice,
however, involves what are usually called operational efforts.
Here the focus is on trying to increase precipitation with
little or no effort made to assess the extent to which the
cloud seeding has in fact increased or decreased precipitation (Farhar, 1975). Attempts to increase the snow pack in
western mountain areas through cloud seeding have been judged
successful under very specific atmospheric conditions. This
application is still a long way from being recognized as
established, however. Run-off from the snow melt is used for
both agricultural and municipal and industrial purposes.
Snow pack augmentation efforts were conducted in several
western states during the winter of 1976-77.

A second type of planned precipitation augmentation is
the seeding of summer storms over agricultural areas. These
efforts, both experimental and operational, have taken place
primarily west of the Mississippi River although one of the
most mentioned experiments was conducted in south Florida
(Hess, 1974). There is little agreement among atmospheric
scientists that the physical processes of seeding of summer-
time clouds are well enough understood to warrant operational
efforts (Farhar, 1976). The Bureau of Reclamation is initia-
ting a large scale experimental program in the high plains
in an effort to answer the question of whether or not precipitation can be increased during the growing season.

There is suggestive evidence that cloud seeding for hail suppression *may* increase precipitation as a by-product, (Changnon, *et al*, 1977). That conclusion also is still very much in doubt, however. What is clear is that operational hail suppression efforts have frequently been the focus of controversy, especially during periods of subnormal rainfall. Opponents argue that hail suppression efforts decrease the amount of precipitation that would have occurred naturally (Farhar and Mewes, 1976; Changnon *et al*, 1977, Haas, 1973).

With the possible exception of cloud seeding to increase snow pack in the mountains, planned weather modification has not yet been demonstrated to be a viable adjustment to drought. Even if the technology was known to be reliable, its application during drought periods would be limited due to the relative absence of "seedable" clouds during such dry periods.

Irrigation represents a hydrological adjustment to drought just as it does during times of normal precipitation. It involves the alteration of the natural hydrological cycle. Roughly, 10% of all farms in the United States use irrigation. Those farming units produce about 20% of the value of all farm crops (Warrick, 1975).

The primary sources for irrigation water are from damming the flow of streams and rivers, direct withdrawal of water from rivers and the pumping of water from underground sources.

Augmenting the supply of irrigation water for one area often, if not always, means that there is less water available for other areas. Sometimes, such reduced availability is of critical importance for an area as in the case of widespread drought while in other cases it has relatively little significance.

B. Conservation of Water. Cultivation practices and water supply protection techniques also have a bearing on the hydrological cycle.

There are a number of practices which, if utilized, will significantly reduce the loss of soil moisture. Among the more widely used practices are summer fallow (allowing the land to lie idle while accumulating moisture), stubble mulching (maintaining the stubble or crop residue on the surface of the soil), strip cropping (alternating strips of growing crops and non-crop areas), contouring and terracing, land leveling and shelterbelts (windbreaks).

Water lost during storage and transportation represents

the largest loss of all. It is lost from water supply systems through seepage, evaporation and transpiration.

As much as 25% of the water supply may be lost through
seepage in unlined canals and ditches. These conduits can be
lined to preclude that loss, but the cost is often considered
exorbitant.

The amount of water lost through evaporation is also
startling. It is estimated that for each acre foot of water
surface in the western United States, four to eight acre feet
of water disappear through evaporation yearly (U.S. Senate
Committee on Interior and Insular Affairs, 1958). Efforts at
developing mono-molecular films to put on the water and thus
reduce evaporation have not met with much success.

Water loss through transpiration is also significant.
Perhaps 20-25 million acre feet of water are lost annually
in this fashion (Howe and Easter, 1971). Water-loving plants
called "phreatophytes" soak up great quantities. These weeds
can be eradicated through the use of chemicals, but the long
term effects on the ecosystem of such eradication are unknown.

Modification of the Agricultural Subsystem.

What adjustments can be made within the agricultural
component? Two categories of adjustments will be reviewed:
altering agricultural characteristics and efforts at spread-
ing/sharing losses and costs.

A. Altering Agricultural Characteristics. One broad-
guage adjustment may be called "operational flexibility."
Under this general heading comes the development and use of
drought resistant crops and livestock, as well as increasing
diversification of crop and livestock production. In some
instances those affected by drought seek alternative employment opportunities. Finally, operational flexibility may
entail a willingness and ability to revise cropping plans in
the face of water shortages.

Land use management is another potential agricultural
adjustment. Since municipal and industrial uses of water
may compete with agricultural use of water, regulating the
rate of land development in agricultural areas would provide
some cushion against a water shortage for agricultural production. Similarly, efforts to stimulate the return of marginal agricultural land to idle lands makes sense especially
in the plains and southwest.

The successful prediction well in advance of drought

periods would make possible the wise use of a number of other
adjustments. At the present time attempts at forecasting
conditions more than a month or two in advance seem to be
little more than guesses. If and when long term forecasts
with significant reliability become available the economic
and social impact of drought can be dampened considerably.

    B. Spread/Share Losses and Costs. This set of adjust-
ments covers, 1) attempts at financial protection, and 2)
relief and rehabilitation programs.

    Financial protection may be attempted through several
adjustments. Since 1938 the Federal Crop Insurance Corporation (FCIC) has made it possible for the farmer to buy all-
hazard crop insurance, but only to the point of recovering
production expenses. Approximately 10% of all U. S. farms
are protected by such insurance. Drought accounts for more
than half of all indemnities paid by the FCIC (U. S. Department of Agriculture, 1970).

    The building up of reserves can provide a similar type
of protection at least for the short run. Financial reserves
and/or reserves of feed and grain can sustain the agricultural
enterprise for a year or two during a drought. If reserves
are not available, credit may be used to budget drought-
induced losses over time.

    Relief and rehabilitation refers to established programs
which may be brought into play when large, widespread losses
occur. For drought, such programs are typically operated by
the Federal government. Some of these special relief efforts
may be put into operation at the discretion of the Secretary
of Agriculture, while others must await a "major disaster"
declaration by the President. Until 1977 at least, these
programs were all reactive. No Federal monies for special
efforts could be made available until after widespread drought
losses occurred. The most common form of assistance is
through low interest loans.

    Figure 3 displays the trend lines for the use of the
various agricultural adjustments to drought in the United
States since 1930.

Adjustments to Drought: Urban Areas

    Urban drought may be seen most readily when there are
significant but unscheduled modifications in water management
practices in an urban area. Demand has outstripped supply to
a greater extent and for a longer period than was anticipated
by the water managers (Warrick, 1975).

TABLE II

ADJUSTMENTS TO DROUGHT: URBAN AREAS

I.   MODIFICATION OF SOURCES AND WATER SYSTEMS

    A.   Alteration of Sources

        Precipitation augmentation

        Desalination

        Waste water reuse

II.   MODIFICATION OF DEMAND

        Land use management

        Economic incentives and penalties

        Legal mechanisms

        "Voluntary" changes in use

           Information
           Conventional practice
           Attitudes and values

        Priorities among competing demands

The range of adjustments to drought in urban areas may
be seen in Table 2.

Modification of Sources and Water Systems.

A. Alteration of Sources of Water for Urban Use. It is
possible to change the sources of urban water through precipitation augmentation, desalination and waste water reuse.
None of these adjustments, however, is being widely used.

The uncertainty regarding the effectiveness of cloud
seeding to augment precipitation means that it is rarely
attempted as a means for easing urban drought. Desalination
as a significant adjustment to urban water shortage is presently feasible, if at all, only for cities located near sea
water and only for emergency use. Very high fuel costs are
a major deterrent.

The failure to reuse waste water as a matter of course
appears to represent a lag between available technology and
practice. There is the possible installation of dual water
systems with the lower quality, reused water being applied
to lawn watering and other irrigation industrial use, the re-
charging of acquifers for irrigation use and for lake-type
recreational use. In addition, storm run-off could be stored
as an additional source of supply. Even home cisterns may
come back into wider use.

B. Alteration of Urban Water Systems. Changes in both
quantity and quality need to be considered here.

Urban drought would have very little significance if
system capacity always was in excess of peak demand. Evidence suggests, however, that frequently that is not the case.
Figure 4 illustrates a tendency which can lead to short-term
severe supply shortage especially if demand increases sharply
during long, but dry periods.

There are a number of other considerations relating to
urban water quantity:

. Estimates of future water availability are often
  inadequate.

. Interbasin transfer of water is becoming more common.
  The use of an urban water "grid system" is largely
  untried, however.

. In poorly maintained transmission and distribution
  systems, as much as 35% of the water is lost in

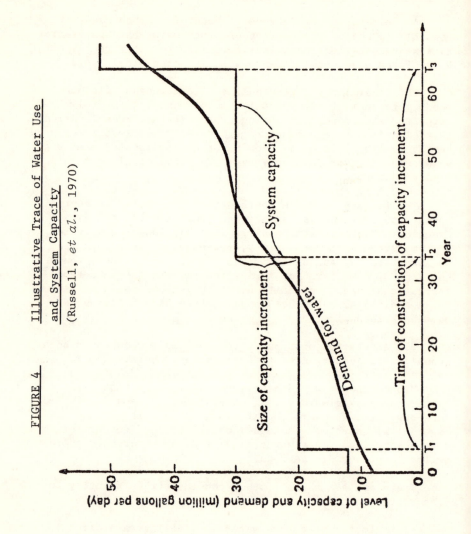

FIGURE 4   Illustrative Trace of Water Use
and System Capacity

(Russell, *et al.*, 1970)

leakage.

. Newly drilled wells are feasible in some instances
  for emergency supply. Such an adjustment will often
  be less expensive than setting up additional surface
  systems.

. Storm run-off in urban areas can be tapped if adequate treatment facilities have been constructed.

. Although the cost is usually very high, hauling
  water by truck and train into a water starved area
  may avoid even greater losses.

. Most urban water systems can be built or enlarged
  only with explicit public approval. This means that
  long range planning with broad based public participation is critical as is adequate information and
  public discussion.

Qualitative considerations come into play as well as
quantity. Taste, appearance and perceived purity of water
are the prime concerns of consumers. The potential use of
recycled water rests largely on these considerations (Metzler
and Russelman, 1968). From a water management point of view,
a drought period may be a propitious time to introduce plans
for the development of waste water or storm run-off reuse.

Modification of Demand.

Almost all of the emphasis in water management has been
on water resources and distribution. There appears to be a
reluctance to seriously consider possible efforts to curb or
shape the demand for urban water.

The following will be considered here: Land use management, economic incentives and penalties, legal mechanisms,
voluntary changes in use levels and priorities and competing
demands.

Land use management involves two broad considerations.
First is the actual use of land (e.g. agriculture, residential, industry, recreation). Different uses require varying
levels of water resources. Second is the total demand for
water within any area. Here total population makes a difference. In January, 1977 the Governor of Hawaii proposed that
Hawaii be declared a "national treasure" and that the concept
be used as a basis for limiting the total number of U. S.
citizens who would be permitted to live in the state. A
potential water shortage was not a major consideration in

this instance. However, the concept is an intriguing one
when considering long term strategies for coping with the
drought hazard.

It is generally recognized that at some point the forces
that limit total water resources will start to curb demand.
Unfortunately, droughts, intervene in the long-term adjustment between supply and demand.

Should "heroic measures" be taken at the taxpayers ex-
pense every time there is a drought?

Should efforts be made to bring the size of the population in an area and the supply of water into a balance that
won't be upset by several years of below normal precipitation?

Or should the current approaches be continued and when
the situation becomes extreme enough, institute temporary
relocation as is done in the face of large-scale riverine
flooding?

Presumably within certain limits water use levels can be
influenced by economic incentives and penalties. Exactly how
elastic the demand for water may be is unclear. Clearly, if
economic factors operate on water use then metering and pricing policies should be the primary tools for curbing demand
during periods of short supply. Most but not all cities,
(e.g. Denver, Colorado) use residential meters. Many cities
and water districts still offer decreasing unit cost as consumption goes up. That pricing policy is still continued in
many areas even when a water shortage is in view. Does such
a pricing policy make sense under any conditions? There has
been little experimentation with variations in pricing policies, or indeed much in-depth analysis. Clearly, there is a
considerable need for careful research on the relation of
pricing policies to water consumption.

There are also various legal mechanisms which relate to
demand level. Water law, especially in the west, is a world
unto itself. Not all uses have equal priority in time of
drought and some cities have higher priority than others for
historical reasons. Local ordinances restricting types of
water use (e.g. prohibiting car washing and lawn sprinkling)
and total consumption per household or business enterprise
are not unusual. Marin County, California is perhaps the
most extreme example in 1977 of radical curtailment of water
consumption enforced by local government. Building code
regulations, if enforced, could also reduce consumption.
Spring loaded faucets, shower heads that restrict the flow of
water, dishwashers and toilet flush boxes that use less water

and the prohibition on swimming pools, all are adjustments
which could be applied through local building code regulations.

In 1977, water managers in many cities attempted to reduce water consumption by urging voluntary reductions in use.
It is not clear whether or not the voluntary approach produced lowered water consumption. During normal periods,
water managers seem not to concern themselves much with the
water use habits of the public. Water conservation is not a
frequent topic in the trickle of communication that goes from
water managers to the public. It is understandably difficult
then to "educate" the public on short notice, to alter conventional practice through a crash public information campaign.
Changes in conventional practice normally come slowly. If
such changes are to come at all, it will most likely be done
by slow, consistent educational efforts in the schools and
through the mass media.

Similarly, relevant attitudes and values are not easily
altered. It is likely that attitudes toward water use are
closely linked to views on community growth, environmental
issues and perhaps attitudes toward consumption in general.
Even a well designed, well financed public information campaign of several weeks duration is not likely to alter significantly basic views on water availability and consumption.

Finally, priorities and competing demands for water
should be considered. It is generally agreed that water for
human consumption should have the highest priority. Thus
some demands have to give way to others when the supply is
inadequate. Some demands for water can be reduced to zero
without irretrievable losses, others cannot (e.g. irrigation
of fruit and nut trees in California's San Joaquin valley).

Interaction Among Adjustments

There are many potential adjustments to the drought hazard. Most of those adjustments could and should be instituted prior to any particular drought period. But as is illustrated in Table 3, the adoption or use of one adjustment may
be linked with availability and adoption of other adjustments.
For example, if agricultural land use regulation which is
enlightened by knowledge of the drought hazard has been applied in a state over a period of years, there will be increasingly less use needed of Federal drought relief programs.
Similarly, if reliable long range climatic prediction becomes
available, financial protection as an adjustment becomes much
more feasible. Also to the extent that irrigation is adopted
there is likely to be less emphasis (adoption) on moisture

TABLE III   Adjustment Interaction

The adoption of: ↓ / Affects the adoption of: →	Cultivation practices	Water supply protection	Weather modification	Irrigation	Operational flexibility	Land use regulation	Prediction/ forecast	Financial protection	Relief & rehabilitation
Cultivation Practices		P	P	R	P			P	–
Water Supply Protection	P	+	R	R	P			P	P
Weather Modification	–		+	P	–			–	P
Irrigation	R	P		R	+	P		+	R
Operational Flexibility	+	P	+		+	P		P	–
Land Use Regulation	+		P	P	R	P		+	–
Prediction/Forecast	R			P	R	P			–
Financial Protection	R		P	P	R	P		P	–
Relief & Rehabilitation						P		P	

blank   No obvious, probable relationship
+   Probable positive relationship
–   Probable negative relationship
R   Complex relationship (+ and/or –)
P   Potential or possible linkage

Both sides of the matrix are included because a dependent-independent relationship is assumed. For example, the adoption of "prediction and forecast" is shown as influencing all other adjustments, but the reverse does not logically hold true.

FIGURE 5   Effects of Adjustments to Drought

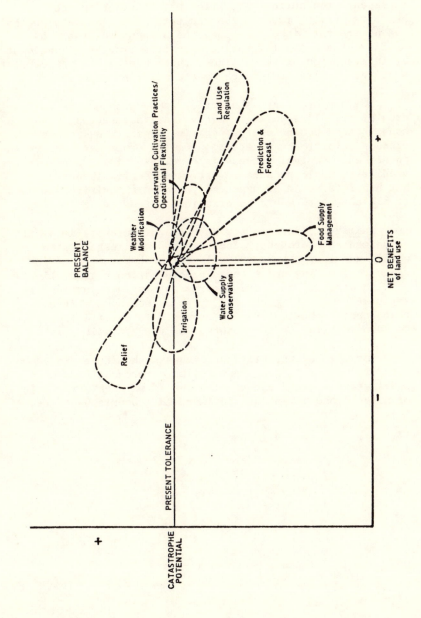

conservation cultivation practices.

Finally, it is important to ask the question, what are the likely consequences for society of leaning heavily on one particular adjustment to drought? Figure 5 portrays that idea in illustrative form. Assume that the vertical line represents the current situation with respect to economic benefits flowing from current adjustments. Assume also that the horizontal line represents the present tolerance by society of a potential catastrophe from drought. The point of intersection of these lines, then, represents the current state of affairs from which we can move into the future.

Now suppose that as a nation we were to emphasize drought relief as an adjustment. Analysis suggests that the consequences would involve negative benefits as well as increased catastrophe potential. On the other hand, heavy emphasis and eventual success in developing long range climate prediction would produce an extremely desirable outcome. Net benefits would be expected to be very positive and catastrophe potential would be drastically reduced.

Summary. There is a wide range of potentially available adjustments to drought. Some are now well established and widely adopted, others are only on the horizon (e.g. long range forecasting and planned precipitation augmentation). As with other geophysical hazards no single adjustment is satisfactory. It is the mix of adjustments or strategies that counts. Most of the adjustments to be effective must be adopted prior to the onset of a drought period.

For the future, heaviest emphasis should be placed on the development of long range climate forecasting and on the application of land use regulations if we seek a reduction of catastrophe potential and improved economic benefits.

REFERENCES

Changnon, Stanley A., *et al*
1977   *Hail Suppression: Impacts and Issues*,
                       Urbana, IL: Illinois State Water Survey.

Farhar, Barbara C.
1975   *"Weather Modification in the United
                       States: A Socio Political Analysis.*
                       Diss., University of Colorado.

Farhar, Barbara C.
1976   "Weather Modification Goes Public,"
                       Journal of Weather Modification, 8
                       (September), pp. 64-76.

Farhar, Barbara C. and Julia Mewes
1976   *Social Acceptance of Weather Modification:
                       The Emergent South Dakota Controversy.*
                       Program on Technology, Environment and
                       Man, Monograph #23, Institute of Behav-
                       ioral Science, University of Colorado.

Haas, J. Eugene
1973   "Social Aspects of Weather Modification."
                       *Bulletin of the American Meteorological
                       Society,* 54 (July), pp. 647-657.

Hess, W. N.
1974   *Weather and Climate Modification.* New
                       York, John Wiley and Sons.

Howe, Charles and K. William Easter
1971   *Interbasin Transfer of Water: Resources
                       for the Future.* Baltimore, MD, Johns
                       Hopkins.

Metzler, D. and H. B. Russelman
1968   "Waste Water Reclamation as a Water
                       Resource." *Journal of the American
                       Water Works Association,* 60, pp. 95-102.

Russell, Clifford S., David G. Arey, and Robert W. Kates
1970   *Drought and Water Supply: Implications
                       of the Massachusetts Experiences for
                       Municipal Planning.* Baltimore, MD,
                       Johns Hopkins.

United States Department of Agriculture
1970   *Economic Considerations in Crop Insurance.*
                       Washington, D. C., United States Govern-
                       ment Printing Office.

United States Senate Committee on Interior and Insular Affairs
1958   *Control of Evaporation Losses.* Committee
                       Print #1. 85th Congress, Second session,
                       Washington, D. C. United States Govern-
                       ment Printing Office.

Warrick, Richard A.
1975   *Drought Hazard in the United States: A
                       Research Assessment.* Program on Tech-
                       nology, Environment and Man, Monograph
                       #NSF-RA-F-75-004. Institute of Behav-
                       ioral Science, University of Colorado.

White, Gilbert F. and J. Eugene Haas
1975   *Assessment of Research on Natural
                       Hazards.* Cambridge, MA, The M.I.T. Press.

ACKNOWLEDGMENT

This paper reflects to a significant degree the perspectives
developed while conducting research on an "Assessment of
Research on Natural Hazards" (NSF Grant GI 32942). The rele-
vant findings and recommendations from that research effort
may be seen in Gilbert F. White and J. Eugene Haas, *Assess-
ment of Research on Natural Hazards,* M.I.T. Press, 1975 and
Richard A. Warrick, *Drought Hazard in the United States: A
Research Assessment,* Institute of Behavioral Science, Re-
search Monograph #004, University of Colorado, Boulder, 1975.
All figures in this text are from Gilbert F. White and J.
Eugene Haas, *Assessment of Research on Natural Hazards,*
M.I.T. Press, 1975.

7

Technological Options for Crop Production in Drought

Norman J. Rosenberg

Introduction

There are numerous technological options which can be used, singly or together, to ameliorate the stresses which droughts impose on agriculture. I will emphasize, primarily, the agricultural aspects of drought amelioration in this paper. The technologies, to be effective, must accomplish at least one of the following four benefits:

1) they must increase the capture of rainfall for storage in the soil or in reservoirs.
2) they must decrease the evaporative loss of stored soil water or water stored in impoundments.
3) they must increase the amounts of water which reach the soil by irrigation or by precipitation enhancement.
4) they must improve the water use efficiency in crop production - i.e., the plant product produced per unit of water consumed.

The first three of the benefits listed above are almost self-explanatory. The concept of water use efficiency is less well known. Plant breeding, microclimatic modification, agronomic management or combinations of these strategies offer possibilities of altering water use efficiency for the better. I will concentrate discussion below on those methods which are directly applicable to crop production under conditions of moisture stress.

Options

Terrace and Contour Farming

The drought of the 1930's gave impetus to the development of many soil and moisture conservation practices. Ter-

Fig. 1. Strip cropped wheat land in the western Great Plains.

race and contour farming was introduced largely after the
1930's. The primary intent of these methods is the reduction
of soil erosion although they are, of course, excellent for
capturing rain and, particularly, for capturing rain which
falls with great intensity. One result of drought is a reduction in the extent and vigor of ground cover. Droughts
can end with the onset of intensive precipitation. Then the
contour and terrace farming methods can be especially important.

Strip Cropping

     Another technique which gained in importance as a result
of the 1930's experience is strip cropping (see Fig. 1).
This method has been used largely in the western Great Plains
for the production of small grains. Half the land is planted
each year while the other half is left fallow to collect
rainfall. Thus a sufficient moisture supply is built for
production of a grain crop every second year. In other
words, it takes two years of rainfall to make a grain crop.
The grain stubble left on the field after harvest, sometimes
until the following spring, should prevent wind erosion.

Stubble Mulch Farming

     Stubble mulch farming gained wide acceptance during the
1950's and 1960's in the western Great Plains. In this system the grain is harvested and the stubble is left in the
field indefinitely. The stubble maintains good soil permea-
bility so that rainfall is absorbed. The stubble also acts
to reduce evaporation from the surface. This technique
definitely improves moisture conservation in the western
Plains region. The main difficulty with both the strip cropping and stubble mulch techniques is the weed growth which
can only be suppressed with specialized equipment or by means
of expensive chemicals.

Minimum Tillage

     Minimum tillage is another technique which has gained
in importance in recent years. When dry soil or soil which
is moist is plowed, the top 15 to 30 cm is exposed to evaporation. However, minimum tillage systems have been designed to slice through the soil, plant the seed, apply fertili-
zer and herbicide - all in one operation without overturning
the soil. Such techniques are not without difficulties,
however. Because of the heavy reliance on herbicides instead
of cultivation, the year after year use of minimum tillage
may create some environmental problems which need to be
solved. Nonetheless, minimum tillage techniques have, quite

Fig. 2. Experimental 2-row tree windbreaks at the University of Nebraska's Agri-cultural Field Laboratory, Mead. Plots within the three tic-tac-toe shaped windbreak systems shown are harvested to measure the influence of the windbreaks on crop yield.

definitely, advanced the art of soil moisture conservation.

Windbreaks

Windbreaks have been used very widely in the Great
Plains and other semi-arid to sub-humid regions such as the
Steppes of the Soviet Union. The major impetus for the widespread systematic planting of windbreaks in the Great Plains
began during the drought of the 1930's when President F. D.
Roosevelt was convinced of the need for a "shelterbelt" project. In its original conception, the Great Plains was to
have been covered north and south, east and west with a close
network of windbreaks. This network was expected to moderate
the climate and to prevent further wind erosion and deterio-
ration of the land. Literally thousands of miles of windbreaks were actually planted - largely, however, in six and
eight row windbreaks which have, after thirty and forty years
of growth, become too dense and overgrown. At this time, in
fact, many farmers in the Great Plains area are removing the
windbreaks planted in an earlier era (1). This removal of
windbreaks is being done because the wide windbreaks occupy
land areas much more valuable now than they were in the
1930's. Windbreaks are being torn out also because many of
the newer type irrigation systems require heavy capital investments and land cannot be spared from production if the
full utilization of the systems is to be achieved. Windbreaks may also interfere with the geometric layout of the
irrigation system.

Despite the fact that certain types of tree windbreaks
are losing ground, there are other kinds which might be sub-
stituted. Research has been done with two row windbreaks,
grown in various species arrangements and orientations with
respect to the wind, in order to determine whether appropriate wind speed reduction can be effected and whether
plants grown in the lee of the windbreak benefit from the
microclimatic modifications provided (Fig. 2). It has already been established that two row windbreaks are more
effective in reducing the force of the wind than are the
overgrown 6 to 8 row types. This is so since a solid wall
breaks the force of the wind and creates a calm zone in the
nearby lee area. However, a short distance away from a
solid windbreak the windspeed returns to normal and the air
may be even more turbulent than in the open. A windbreak
which is partly porous to the wind is much more effective
in spreading snow evenly in winter and in maintaining a more
uniformly lower windspeed over the sheltered crop (2).

Another alternative to the large dense windbreak is
shown in Fig. 3. These are windbreaks composed of double

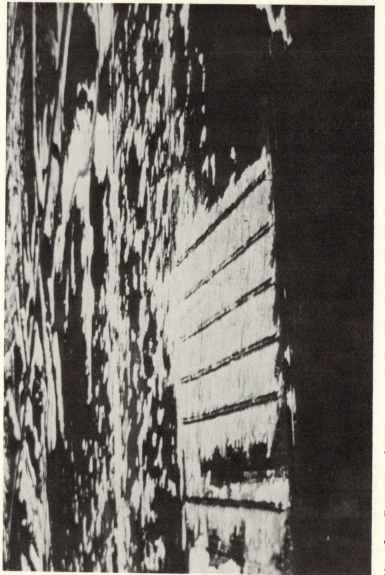

Fig. 3. Two row wheatgrass windbreaks during a Montana winter. The wheatgrass is effective in retaining snow which provides soil moisture for the growth in spring of winter wheat.

rows of wheat grass used to shelter land used in small grain
production. Snow has been swept by the wind from the sur-
rounding areas but is held in the sheltered areas. Aase and
Siddoway (3) report significantly improved grain production
where this system has been used due to the improved water
supply from snow trapping and to the moderate microclimate
created by the wheat grass barrier during the grain growing
season.

Other types of vegetative windbreaks -- corn to shelter
soybeans, corn to shelter sugarbeets and other combinations
of tall and short intertilled crops can create a microclimate
very conducive to the growth of the sheltered plant as well
as the sheltering plant (4, 5). For example, Brown and
Rosenberg (5) report the use of corn in double rows to shelter irrigated sugarbeets. After three years of experimentation the yield of sheltered sugarbeets was 16% greater than
in the open despite the loss of area to the corn windbreaks.
The windbreaks themselves yielded 15.5 ton/hectare of corn --
an extremely good yield for western Nebraska. The combination of benign microclimate for the sugarbeets and better
exposure of the corn to sun and to wind -- which may have
enhanced turbulent transport of CO_2 to the crop -- probably
explains the excellent yield performance.

Irrigation

Irrigation has developed very rapidly in much of the
Great Plains. In Nebraska, particularly during the last half
dozen years, growth has been dramatic. As shown in Fig. 4,
surface irrigated land area had grown slowly from the beginning of the century until the mid 1950's. In 1950 a total
of one million acres (~ 400,000 hectare) were under irrigation -- about half with gravity flow water from reservoirs
and lakes and the other half with well water. Irrigated
acreage increased at a more or less constant rate until 1965.
Then the rate of irrigation development began to increase
radically in Nebraska. Since 1974, occurrences of drought
have given additional impetus to the process, so that growth
projected in 1971 has exceeded all expectation.

Irrigation has, during the drought years of this decade,
buffered Nebraska against the loss of crop production. The
average yield of irrigated corn in Nebraska is about 100
bushels per acre (6.3 ton/ha) and, as shown in Fig. 5, this
production has been fairly constant. The average annual
production from irrigated land has, of course, risen because
of the increase in land area irrigated. Corn on dryland
yields an average of 30-35 bushels per acre (1.9 - 2.2 ton/
ha). During the drought of 1974, the average yield fell to
25 bushels per acre (1.6 ton/ha). Yet total corn production

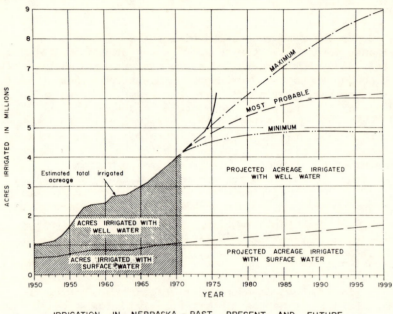

IRRIGATION IN NEBRASKA – PAST, PRESENT AND FUTURE

UNIVERSITY OF NEBRASKA – CONSERVATION AND SURVEY DIVISION — V.H.DREESZEN, DIRECTOR   Drafted by
F. Wickenkamp

Fig. 4. Acreage of lands in Nebraska irrigated with waters
of surface and subsurface origin as of 1971. Pro-
jections of maximum irrigation development expected
by 1976 were exceeded by 1 million acres.

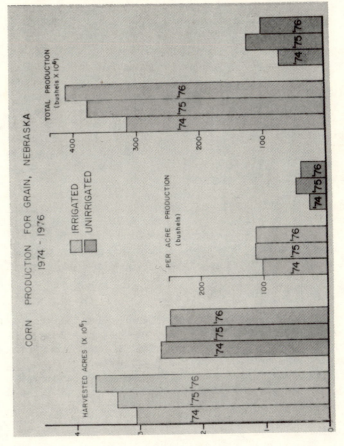

Fig. 5. Components of the total corn production for grain on dryland and under irrigation in Nebraska, 1974-1976.

has remained nearly constant because of irrigation which has
made up for loss of dryland production.

The newly irrigated land area is irrigated almost entirely from ground water. Obviously the current growth rate
cannot be sustained. Land for irrigation will run out in
another few years if the exponential growth rate continues.
Recharge of Nebraska's vast underground water resource -- a
barrel which some though too big to ever go empty -- has
definitely not kept pace with the rate of increase in irrigation and the increased water demands due to the drought in
the 1970's. Therefore, the potential for irrigation to
alleviate the stresses due to drought may be approaching its
limits.

Were it possible to divert some water from intensive
irrigation for the supplemental irrigation of what are now
dryland areas, total production might be increased even more.
An application of one or two irrigations, at critical times
during the growing season, might lead to major increases in
production per unit of land area. Such a tactic would provide a degree of drought-proofing.

To accomplish this reallocation or temporary diversion
of water would not be simple. Most of the new center pivot
irrigation systems are very expensive -- currently about
$50,000 of investment to irrigate a quarter section of land
(160 acres; ~ 65 ha)(15). Nor are these systems moved easily
from place to place although movement is certainly possible
and is practiced by some irrigators.

Older irrigation systems, such as the so-called "skid-
tow" now thought obsolete by some, may be useful for drought
proofing. In this system, aluminum laterals on which sprink-
lers are mounted are pulled back and forth from field to
field by tractor. Only the availability of pipe, the availability of water or the unsuitability of the topography need
limit the mobility of these systems. Other engineering de-
signs which permit greater mobility and flexibility of
sprinkler irrigation systems are certainly needed at this
time.

Great improvements have also been made in recent years
in the design and operation of gravity flow furrow irrigation systems. A design criterion permitting the runoff of
25% of the applied irrigation water was acceptable a decade
ago. It is no longer necessary to over-irrigated in order
to wet the down-field end of the furrow since irrigation
engineers have developed systems of reuse (or capture) pits
into which the runoff flows for return by pumps back into
the upslope head of the system. Now, no water need be lost

from gravity flow fields except by evaporation.

Weather Modification

A number of studies have shown that, were it possible to increase rainfall in the Great Plains by 10 to 20% immensely important economic benefits would result, e.g. (6). Research to date, however, has not demonstrated that rainfall augmentation on this scale is really possible. Unfortunately, in times of true drought stress, seedable clouds are very rare. In eastern Nebraska during the drought of 1974, skies were virtually cloudless for nearly 60 days. Rainfall enhancement during the non-growing season might be helpful. Again, however, in the Great Plains region it has not been demonstrated that consistent rainfall augmentation is possible.

Plant Breeding and Biophysics

The job of the plant breeder is to adapt crop plants in ways which fit them better to the general environment and to the occasional extremes of stress caused by weather, disease and pests. Traditional methods of plant breeding are being used to achieve these ends. For example, soybeans tend to be indeterminate in their growth pattern. The plant continues its vegetative growth for a long part of the season. New flowers are produced for a long period and, hence, many soybean varieties tend to become quite tall. We know from fluid dynamics and micrometeorology that the windspeed increases logarithmically with height above the surface. Hence, a tall plant encounters greater wind speed than does a short plant. More warm, dry air moves across the leaves of the taller plants. This can induce moisture stress in the plant which leads to loss of turgor, stomatal closure and wilting. It would seem a logical strategy, all other factors being equal, to breed for shorter plants in regions which are subjected to strong drying winds. Breeders are developing soybeans of 30-40 cm in height (down from 100 cm) which appear as productive as the longer indeterminate varieties.

Changes in leaf architecture may also contribute to the plant's ability to survive a dry, hot spell. A smooth leaf is not as likely to preserve water as a crinkled leaf which tends to create small pockets of still air.

One may find examples, however, of adaptations to environment which have been unsuccessful. One short variety of wheat, very productive in good years, has been found lacking under moisture stress since the short growth habit is associated with a root zone of very limited

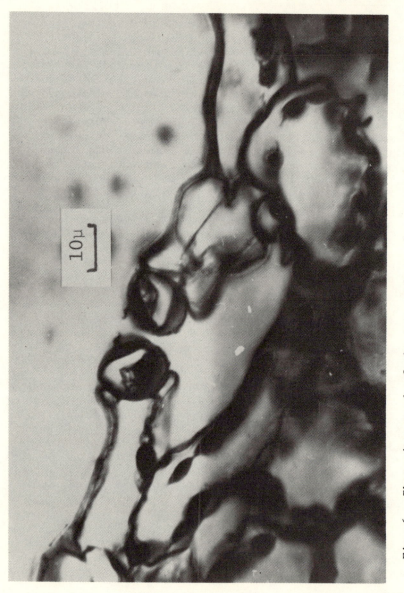

Fig. 6. Photomicrograph of the top surface of a sugar beet leaf showing epidermal and mesophyll cells, guard cells and sub-stomatal cavity.

depth.

Thus we see that the problems of breeding plants which can avoid or resist environmental stress are complicated. Fundamental information is needed to support breeding efforts which aim to optimize the design of new crop varieties suited to drought conditions.

A Biophysical Approach to Drought Proofing

We begin with Ohm's Law

$$I = \frac{V}{R} \tag{1}$$

which indicates that the flow of current in an electrical system, I, is proportional to the voltage or driving force, V, working against a resistance, R. A simple analogy of Ohm's Law can be used to describe evapotranspiration from a plant leaf. Figure 6 is a photomicrograph of a stomate and the substomatal cavity in a sugarbeet leaf. Air within the stomatal cavity is normally moist - close to 100% relative humidity, unless the plant is approaching a wilted condition. Water vapor must pass through the stomate into the air above in order for transpiration to occur. A resistance imposed by the stomates (the stomatal resistance, r_s) limits the rate of diffusion of vapor from the stomate into the air. An integration of the stomatal resistances over whole leaves and entire crop surfaces yields the canopy resistance, r_c. Water vapor molecules, after emerging from the leaf, must diffuse through the air to reach a particular level above the surface. The air exerts a resistance to diffusion (the aerial resistance, r_a). On the basis of these elementary facts we can prepare an analogy of Ohm's Law for transpiration (in terms of the flux of latent heat LE) from a crop canopy

$$LE = (\rho_a \frac{L\varepsilon}{P}) \; \frac{e_s - e_a}{r_s + r_c} \tag{2}$$

where ρ_a is the density of air, ε is the ratio of the mole weights of water and air, P is the atmospheric pressure, L is the latent heat of vaporization and E the quantity of water evaporated. The diffusion of water vapor from leaf to air is driven by the difference in vapor pressures between the substomatal cavity and the air ($e_s - e_a$).

Of the parameters in equation (2) e_s (the vapor pressure in the substomatal cavity) is the most difficult to know. A model was developed by Brown and Rosenberg (7) which permits solution of equation (2) by a substitution for e_s which is based upon energy balance considerations (16).

Fig. 7. An experiment in which portions of a soybean field were coated with Celite in order to increase the albedo, reduce the net radiant energy and reduce evapotranspiration.

$$LE = \frac{\left\{\left[f\left(\frac{(R_n - S - LE)r_a}{C_p \, \rho_a} + T_a\right) - e_a\right] \frac{M_w/M_a}{P} L\rho_a\right\}}{(r_a + r_s)}$$ (3)

Thus the model permits prediction of the transpiration rate from a knowledge of the stomatal (or canopy) and aerial resistances and the ambient air temperature and vapor pressure. It is also necessary in order to use this equation to know the sum of the net radiation and the soil heat flux.

Examination of equation (3) indicates, simply, that transpiration will increase with increasing air temperature and increasing net radiation. With increasing humidity of the air, transpiration will decrease. As the stomatal (or canopy) resistance rises, transpiration decreases. The effect of increasing aerial resistance, r_a, is more complex since it appears in both the numerator and denominator of equation (3).

Verma and Rosenberg (8) have simplified the data requirements for use of the model by developing functional relations of r_s on irradiance and r_a on windspeed. Detailed predictions of the influence of windbreaks, antitranspirant chemicals reflectant materials on the transpiration have been published by Rosenberg and Brown (9). These predictions have been verified in field studies (10, 11, 12).

One case in point: the model predicted that reduced net radiation should reduce transpiration under the general environmental conditions which prevail in the eastern Great Plains region. Net radiation can be reduced by increasing the albedo of a crop. In experiments conducted at Mead, Nebraska during the period 1969-1973 soybeans were coated with kaolinite and with Celite (a diatomaceous earth product of the Johns-Manville Company) (See Fig. 7). Figures 8 and 9 indicate the effects of the Celite reflectants on the evapotranspiration by two cultivars of soybean treated with the reflectant. As the solar radiation flux density increases in the morning, treated soybeans diverge from the untreated soybeans in transpiring considerably less water. Savings in transpiration were in the order of 10-15%.

Water saved by this method will eventually be consumed by the soybeans. However, the crop will be healthier and might conceivably survive a dry spell while the untreated plants wilt or die. Regular use of reflectants by Great Plains farmers is unlikely in the near future because of the costs of materials and application. However, the use of such a tactic may not be uneconomic in times of drought. Further,

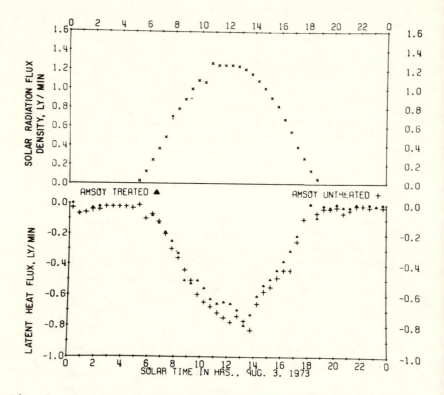

Fig. 8.   Solar radiation flux density and evapotranspiration
(as latent heat flux) from Amsoy soybeans treated
with Celite to increase albedo of the crop.

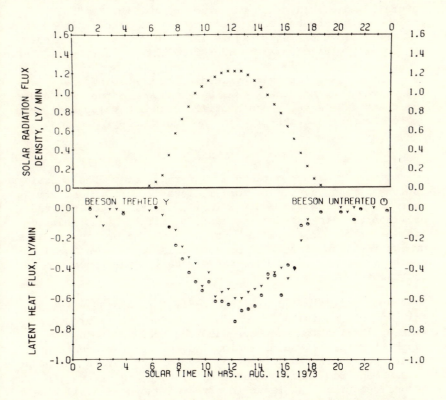

Fig. 9. Same as Fig. 8 for the Beeson cultivar of soybeans.

in the developing countries, where labor intensive operations
may be desireable, applications of reflectant materials by
hand dusting techniques may be perfectly feasible.

The principles demonstrated by agricultural meteorolo-
gists and biophysicists have not gone entirely unnoticed.
While we have been trying to artificially reflectorize
plants, plant breeders in Montana (13) have been developing
naturally more reflectant varieties of barley. A "golden"
isogene of barley has been found to have a higher albedo than
its green isogenic lines. Thus far results do not indicate
any lower yields than are produced by the ordinary varieties.

Thus we see that biophysicists, agrometeorologists,
plant breeders and others can, by working together and apply-
ing their skills and the scientific method, develop realistic
approaches for drought-proofing agricultural production.

Summary

I have tried to catalog a wide range of technological
options already available for amelioration of drought stress.
These methods include contour farming, strip cropping, use
of windbreaks to capture snow and for microclimate modification. Certain of these methods have been in use for decades;
others for centuries. But because they are old and good
practice in good times does not disqualify them from use in
bad times.

Good soil stewardship is essential to avoid excessive
soil and productivity losses when the inevitable droughts
strike. Irrigation has increased the overall productive
capability of the Plains region and much of the mountain
west. But limits to irrigation development may be approaching in many regions. Engineering systems and strategies are
needed such that, at least in times of drought, available
water can be spread over larger areas of land to yield a
greater total production. Supplemental irrigation, where
feasible, should increase the stability of agriculture and
agricultural industry in drought affected regions.

Weather modification -- rainmaking -- could be very
important. However, evidence is not yet at hand which shows
that effective systems of rainmaking can be conducted under
the meteorological conditions of the Great Plains. Rainmaking to increase snow pack in the mountainous regions may
be more feasible as a drought proofing technique.

Biophysical models can provide guidance for the development of new architecture for the crops which grow in regions

where moisture stress is frequent. These models, of which I have discussed only one rudimentary example, also provide guidance for the development of new microclimate modification techniques and new agronomic management methods which can also help to ameliorate the impact of drought.

References and Notes

(1) Griffith, P. 1976. Introduction of the problems. In, R. W. Tinus, ed., Proc. Symp. on Shelterbelts on the Great Plains. Great Plains Agric. Council Publ. No. 78 (pps 3-7).

(2) Van Eimern, J., R. Karschon, L. A. Razumova and G. W. Robertson. 1964. Windbreaks and Shelterbelts. World Meteorol. Organ. Tech. Note No. 59, 199 pp.

(3) Aase, J. K. and F. H. Siddoway. 1974. Tall wheatgrass barriers and winter wheat response. Agric. Meteorol. 13:321-338.

(4) Radke, J. K. 1976. The use of annual wind barriers for protecting row crops. In, R. W. Tinus, ed., Proc. Symp. on Shelterbelts on the Great Plains. Great Plains Agric. Council Publ. No. 78 (pps 79-87).

(5) Brown, K. W. and N. J. Rosenberg. 1972. Shelter-effects on microclimate, growth and water use by irrigated sugar beets in the Great Plains. Agric. Meteorol. 9:241-263.

(6) Chagnon, S. A. , Jr. 1971. Evaluation of potential benefits of weather modification on agriculture. Final report to USD Interior, Bureau of Reclamation on Contract 14-06-D-6843, Oct. 31, 1971.

(7) Brown, K. W. and N. J. Rosenberg. 1973. A resistance model to predict evapotranspiration and its application to a sugar beet field. Agron. J. 65:341-347.

(8) Verma, S. B. and N. J. Rosenberg. 1977. The Brown-Rosenberg resistance model of crop evapotranspiration modified: Tests in an irrigated sorghum field. Agron. J. 69:332-335.

(9) Rosenberg, N. J. and K. W. Brown. 1973. Measured and modelled effects of microclimate modification on evapotranspiration by irrigated crops in a region of strong sensible heat advection. Proc. Symp. on Plant Response to Climatic Factors. Ecology and Conservation 5:539-

546, UNESCO, Paris.

(10) Miller, D. R., N. J. Rosenberg and W. T. Bagley. 1973.
     Soybean water use in the shelter of a slat-fence wind-
     break. Agric. Meteorol. 11:405-418.

(11) Hales, T. A. 1970. The effect of antitranspirant mat-
     erials on the radiation balance and evapotranspiration
     in an irrigated alfalfa field. Progress Report 83,
     Dept. of Hort. and Forestry, Univ. of Nebraska on
     Nebraska Water Resources Research Inst. Project A-001-
     NEB (pp 180).

(12) Baradas, M. W. 1974. Reflectorized soybeans: Growth,
     production and longwave radiation balance. Progress
     Report 108, Dept. of Hort. and Forestry, Univ. of Neb-
     raska on National Science Foundation Grant GA-24137
     (pp 147).

(13) Ferguson, H., C. S. Cooper, J. H. Brown and R. F.
     Eslick. 1972. Effect of leaf color, chlorophyll con-
     centration and temperature on photosynthetic rates of
     isogenic barley lines. Agron. J. 64:671-673.

(14) Published as paper no. 5432 , Journal Series, Nebraska
     Agricultural Experiment Station.

(15) Because of their circular arrangement center pivot sys-
     tems actually irrigate less than the full 160 acres in
     a quarter section. From about 128-146 acres can be
     irrigated depending on the system design.

(16) For details of the model see Brown and Rosenberg (7).
     The solution to eq. 3 requires iteration. First approx-
     imations of the value of LE are obtainable by methods
     described in reference (7).

8

State and Federal
Responses to the
1977 Drought

A. Berry Crawford

Introduction

The areal extent of the 1977 drought is unprecedented.
Over 2,200 counties in the United States--over four-fifths
of the Nation's total--have been designated as "emergency
drought areas" during 1977 for purposes of federal relief.
The broad geographical scope of this drought is strikingly
portrayed by the weekly Palmer drought index maps published
by the National Oceanic and Atmospheric Administration
(NOAA). During the spring months of the year, moderate to
extreme drought measurements (-2 to -9 on the Palmer scale)
covered large portions of the west, midwest, and north
central regions of the nation. Going into the summer,
drought conditions extended through almost all of the
southeastern states, and only areas of the midwest were
beginning to experience relief. Figure 1 illustrates the
national drought situation as of August 20, 1977.

The impacts of the 1977 drought have likewise been
pervasive and severe. Many communities have experienced
acute water shortages and have been forced to undertake
emergency measures ranging from mandatory rationing to the
drilling of new wells and the transport of water by tank
truck or temporary surface pipelines. Due to impaired
range conditions and shortages of hay and drinking water--
conditions directly attributable to the drought--many
cattlemen have been forced to sell even their foundation
stock at depressed prices, and now face bankruptcy. And
even though the U.S. was expected at this writing to have
its third largest crop harvest in history--an anomaly to be
discussed below--many farmers are facing economic disaster
because soil moisture was insufficient for germination, or
because the rains didn't come soon enough or additional
water couldn't be supplied from groundwater or reservoir
storage at critical growing stages.

FIGURE 1

DROUGHT SEVERITY
(PALMER INDEX)

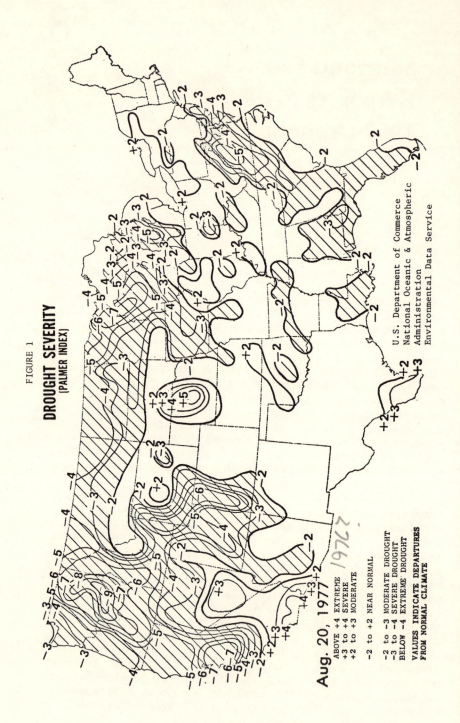

Aug. 20, 1977

ABOVE +4 EXTREME
+3 to +4 SEVERE
+2 to +3 MODERATE

−2 to +2 NEAR NORMAL

−2 to −3 MODERATE DROUGHT
−3 to −4 SEVERE DROUGHT
BELOW −4 EXTREME DROUGHT

VALUES INDICATE DEPARTURES
FROM NORMAL CLIMATE

U.S. Department of Commerce
National Oceanic & Atmospheric
Administration
Environmental Data Service

The impact does not end here. Other problems stemming from the drought include ski areas with little or no snow, high and dry marinas, aluminum production cutbacks from shortages of hydroelectric power, curtailed timber harvests, fisheries losses, devastating forest fires, grasshopper infestations, wind erosion, destruction of wildlife habitat, strain on financial institutions through foreclosures and loan demands, unemployment, and loss of revenue to state and local governments.

As the drought became more and more evident during the winter months of 1977 and dire predictions were being sounded, the level of private and public concern rose sharply and led to remarkable state and federal responses. Front page newspaper accounts, featured articles in leading news-magzines, TV documentaries, and drought conferences and meetings became commonplace. Over 60 drought-related bills were introduced in Congress, including those which made up the President's $844 million "drought package," and many existing federal programs were re-tooled and mobilized to deal with the drought's impending problems. The result was the most expensive and one of the most rapidly mounted and best coordinated relief effòrts in the Nation's history. The states responses were ño less impressive, with emergency powers being granted to governors, scores of drought-related bills being introduced in state legislatures, and local, state, and multistate task forces being formed to develop plans and programs for dealing with the expected problems.

Review of States Responses

Because of the broad geographical extent of the winter drought and the perceived severity of impacts, the states wasted little time in developing drought management strategies and mobilizing needed resources. In California and several upper midwestern states--states which had already experienced drought conditions for a year or more--existing programs were extended and new ones instituted. All of the states looked to the federal government for timely and effective assistance.

Multilateral States Responses

The meeting of the eleven-state Western States Water Council in Portland, Oregon on January 28 evidenced the states' growing concern with drought conditions. It was decided at this meeting that the Western States Water Council should publish and broadly disseminate a weekly bulletin entitled Western Drought Conditions: 1977 to document drought conditions and report on key state and

federal actions taken to deal with these conditions.
Also indicative of an early and widespread concern with the
deepening drought was the appearance of Colorado's Governor
Richard D. Lamm, at the January 20 meeting of the Western
Governors' Task Force on Regional Policy Management to
discuss actions that might be taken on a multistate basis.

These two meetings led to another meeting in Denver
(February 20) attended by Interior Secretary Andrus and the
governors of fourteen western states (four other states were
represented by governors' representatives). Called because
previous efforts on the part of the states to ascertain the
extent of federal preparedness for dealing with drought had
ended in frustration and confusion--a situation understand-
able in view of the fact that the change of Administrations
was just underway--this meeting ended with three notable
agreements. First, the Secretary of the Interior would
seek the appointment of a White House-level drought
coordinator to be located in the Executive Office of the
President. Second, each governor would appoint a state
drought coordinator. Third, the governors would meet one
week later at the annual meeting of the National Governors'
Conference in Washington, D. C. to consider taking concrete
steps on a multilateral basis for dealing with the drought
and its impacts.

All three of these agreements led to early and effective
actions. On February 22, the President appointed Jack
Watson, Cabinet Secretary and Assistant for Intergovernmental
Relations, as the Federal Drought Coordinator. The meeting
of the western governors on February 27 at the annual
National Governors'Conference resulted in the formation of
the twenty-one state Western Regional Drought Action Task
Force (WRDATF), [1] chaired by Governor Lamm and staffed by
the Western States Water Council and the Institute for Policy
Research. The state drought coordinators, appointed by the
governors following the February 20 meeting in Denver, were
designated as the governors' alternates on the WRDATF.

The WRDATF has played a significant role in helping
effect cooperative federal-state relations, providing
information to the states on the status of new and existing
federal programs, representing states' interests before
Congress and the Administration, coordinating and exchanging
information on state actions, and organizing special studies
related to drought problems. Principal milestones and
achievements in the work of the WRDATF are noted below:

- Weekly publication of <u>Western Drought Conditions:
  1977</u> by the Western States Water Council.
  (Beginning February 1)

● WRDATF staff worked with four federal agency
  personnel (representing the Federal Disaster
  Assistance Administration, the Bureau of Reclamation,
  the Department of Agriculture, and the Corps of
  Engineers) dispatched by Jack Watson to the office
  of the Western States Water Council in Salt Lake
  City to provide early federal-state coordination.
  (March 15-24)

● Meeting of the WRDATF staff and alternates in Salt
  Lake City to review the proposed $844 million White
  House "drought package," exchange information on
  problems and actions of the individual states, and
  refine the mission of the WRDATF (March 27).

● Assignment of the Director of the Institute for
  Policy Research to the office of the Federal Drought
  Coordinator to monitor and report on Administration
  and Congressional drought initiatives and to prepare
  a "directory of federal drought assistance."
  (March 29-May 13)

● Meeting of the WRDATF staff and alternates in Denver
  to review status of the White House "drought
  package" and form working groups to deal with issues
  and problems in the areas of crops and irrigation;
  livestock and rangeland; fish, wildlife and recreation; energy, business, and industry; and Task Force
  Management. (April 27)

● Publication and distribution of 6,000 copies of the
  Directory of Federal Drought Assistance: 1977 by the
  Department of Agriculture for the WRDATF. (June 3)

● Assignment of a member of the Utah Department of
  Agriculture to USDA on a temporary duty assignment
  to coordinate federal and state agricultural programs. (month of July)

● Initiation and organization of efforts leading to the
  passage and signing of S. 1935 which gives the
  Secretary of the Interior authority to reallocate
  funds from the "water bank" program to other programs
  (e.g., states grants) as authorized by S. 925.
  (S. 1935 signed by the President on August 17)

● Organization by the Institute for Policy Research of
  invitational workshops on drought research needs
  (in cooperation with the National Science Foundation
  and the Corps of Engineers' Institute for Water

Research), drought economic impacts (in cooperation
with the Economic Development Administration and the
Economic Research Service), and emergency preparedness (in cooperation with the National Science
Foundation, the National Governors'Conference, and
the Council of State Planning Agencies) held on
October 14-15, December 1-2, and December 8-9,
respectively.

Before considering the actions taken by individual
states to combat the 1977 drought, several other multistate
coalitions deserve mention. One is the work of the National
Governors' Conference Subcommittee on Water Resources,
chaired by Governor Scott Matheson of Utah. Another is the
Pacific Northwest Regional Drought Task Force established by
the Pacific Northwest Regional Commission on March 8, 1977.
Nearly $850,000 has been provided by this regional commission
for cloud seeding and other drought-related projects within
the States of Washington, Oregon, and Idaho. Several of the
major public interest groups--most notably the U.S.
Conference of Mayors and the National Association of Counties
--have also played important roles in assisting constituent
groups to cope with the drought.

Individual States Responses

Although the federal government and several multistate
task forces have provided substantial assistance, the states
themselves and their political subdivisions have served as
the principal instrumentalities for managing the current
drought. Since it is not possible to review here the drought
mitigation activities of all of the many affected states, it
will be instructive to touch on the responses of three of the
hardest-hit states, California, Washington, and South Dakota.

California [2]

Precipitation and runoff in most of Northern California
are the lowest in over 100 years of record. Part of the
extremely low runoff (15 to 25 percent of normal in the
Sacramento, Feather, American, and San Joaquin basins) can
be attributed to the low (30 percent of normal) precipitation
in 1976. The domestic [3], agricultural [4], power [5],
wildland fire, and other impacts of these extreme drought
conditions are severe.

Some of the major efforts undertaken by the State of
California to deal with these impacts include:

- Establishment of a Drought Information Center by the Department of Water Resources in January and an intensive program to disseminate information and educational materials on water conservation.

- Establishment on March 4, 1977 of the Governor's Drought Emergency Task Force and regional advisory groups.

- Completion by the Governor's Drought Emergency Task Force of an assistance directory that fixes responsibility and provides State contact points in solving drought-related problems.

- Requirement by the Governor's Drought Emergency Task Force that all State agencies and departments prepare contingency plans for coping with a possible third year of extreme drought.

- Establishment of mandatory water rationing programs by 103 cities and communities (more than 25 percent of the State's population) and voluntary programs in another 100 cities and communities as a result of a State request that local water agencies develop specific drought management plans.

- Enactment of special State legislation to provide low cost loans to communities for emergency facilities, waive the requirement of meeting State environmental quality standards in the implementation of certain drought projects, negate the requirement for water districts to hold special bond elections prior to encumbering federal financial obligations for drought projects, and provide water saving kits to the general public in selected areas.

- Adoption of water conservation programs in State agency operations.

- Emergency exchanges of water by water districts.

- State water trucks made available for water hauling to farmers in Sonoma, Marin, and other counties.

- Initiation of State cloud seeding programs on the North Coast and Sacramento Valley watersheds.

- Organization by State agencies of 13 community and two industrial water conferences.

- Installed temporary rock barriers to direct water flow and enhance water quality in the Sacramento-San Joaquin delta channels.

- Coordination of local government and water districts for the emergency installation of a 6 mile pipeline across the Richmond-San Raphael Bridge to provide 10,000 acre-feet (3,260,000,000 gallons) of water.

Washington [6]

The State of Washington, like its sister States, Oregon and Idaho, has been caught up in its worst drought in history. In aggregate economic terms, the drought was expected to result in a $300-400 million reduction in the Gross State Product, and employment losses were expected to be high. Most of the losses can be traced to poor agricultural and timber harvests and to cutbacks in the aluminum industry which supplies nearly 80 percent of the nation's aluminum needs. To cope with these and other problems--problems created by water shortages in some 77 communities, for example--the State has:

- Established the Ad Hoc Executive Water Emergency Committee, a group consisting of 12 state agencies, 7 federal agencies, and a tri-county commission to coordinate drought-related activities within the State, assist parties afflicted by the drought to obtain available relief and assistance, and organize local government workshops and information dissemination programs.

- Played in active role in obtaining federal drought legislation; S. 925 (the "Water Bank" Bill) was introduced by Senator Henry Jackson of Washington.

- Joined with Idaho and Oregon through the Pacific Northwest Regional Commission to create the Pacific Northwest Regional Drought Task Force; some $250,000 of the available Title V funds were utilized in cloud seeding and other drought projects in the State of Washington.

- Organized a "Save Electricity-Save Jobs" campaign to encourage voluntary conservation.

- Enacted legislation providing up to $18 million in State funds to help finance emergency agricultural water supply projects, and up to $15 million for municipal water supply projects.

South Dakota [7]

South Dakota, like North Dakota and Minnesota, began
1977 with three years of severe drought behind it.   The years
of 1976 and 1974 were the second and third driest in the
State's history, respectively.   The situation in the summer
of 1976 was described thus: "Three years of drought had left
pastures barren, crops were a failure due to an absence of
soil moisutre, the spring alfalfa had been lost to a frost,
and there was insufficient forage to maintain foundation
livestock herds." [8]   By the end of the year, the State
experienced forced selldowns of cattle (more than 50 percent
in 27 counties), extensive crop losses (more than 50 percent
in 48 counties), costly wind erosion losses (in excess of $9
million), and severe water supply problems in many communities.

Serious drought conditions persisted in the State
through May of 1977 (average precipitation for May was 50
percent of normal), but fortunately plentiful amounts of rain
fell during the early months of summer and the extreme grip
of the drought appeared to have been broken in many areas
of the State, especially in the south (see the August Palmer
index values on page 2).   The welcome rains contributed to
generally good harvests and relieved (although, as of this
writing, not entirely) the acute water shortages that persisted for more than two years in many areas of the State's
rural communities.

South Dakota has effectively mobilized its forces to
deal with the prolonged drought.   Some noteworthy milestones
in the State and local response are:

- The County Extension Service, Cooperative Extension
  Service, and other agencies mounted extensive public
  education and information programs.

- Several offices were established and funded to
  assess the impacts of the drought and provide information on available assistance programs, including
  the Drought Assistance and Research Office
  (staffed by 11 staff members on temporary duty
  assignments from existing State agencies) and the
  earlier interagency Drought Task Force administered
  within the Department of Natural Resources.
  Drought assessments were conducted on the State's
  nine Indian reservations as well as in many counties.

- Extensive emergency legislation was passed: $29,219
  for staff increases in the Division of Water Rights

to expedite the processing of water rights applications: $40,000 for additional water test wells
(again to expedite the processing of water rights
applications); legislation authorizing the Governor
to relax the weight, height, width, and taxation
statutes for trucks hauling livestock feed; $1
million in supplemental funds to the Rural Rehabilitation Program for direct loans to low income
families, livestock loans, and farm managment
education; and $2.8 million for aid to drought im-
pacted school districts.

• Other measures taken by the State include: initia-
ting a county grasshopper control program; relaxing
highway rights-of-way for hay mowing; modifying
certification requirements to make farmers and
ranchers eligible for food stamps; running advertisements in out-of-state publications to obtain herd
placement; maintaining hay and pasture availability
listings; and holding a number of drought conferences.

The Southeastern States

    As mentioned earlier, the southeastern states did not
begin to experience serious drought condtions until mid-
spring. Virginia was the first State to have counties
designated as emergency drought areas, followed by Georgia,
West Virginia, Maryland, Florida, North Carolina, South
Carolina, and Mississippi. Pastures and livestock have
generally been hard-hit, and some crop harvests were behind
normal. In Georgia, for example, corn was rated poor;
cotton and peanuts mostly fair; and pastures poor to mostly
fair. (9) As in the west and midwest, the drought has also
threatened municipal water supplies and has let to rationing
in some communities.

    In organizing to deal with the drought, the south-
eastern states have "gone it alone"; no multistate organization comparable to the Western Regional Drought Action
Task Force has been formed or called upon for the exchange
of information and technical assistance, or for the aggre-
gation of political power to influence federal actions.
While each State has detailed personnel and developed plans
for managing drought problems, the response has been mostly
that of a unilateral effort by each State to secure federal
relief. In large measure, this response has been "political," taking the form of phone calls and letters from elected State officials (governors, congressmen, and senators)
to the secretaries and administrators of the various
agencies providing needed assistance.

Review of the Federal Response

Soon after his appointment as the Federal Drought
Coordinator by President Carter on February 22, 1977, Jack
Watson and his assistants, Walter Kallaur and Rodgers
Stewart made two sets of inquiries--one of governors asking
them to describe drought problems within their states and to
suggest what they considered appropriate federal responses
and what the federal response had been to date; the other of
the top administrators of the federal agencies asking them
to describe existing drought-related programs within their
agencies and to summarize complaints they have received on
the adequacy of these programs.

In order to gain a sense of the extent and severity of
the drought from a national perspective and a rough estimate of the magnitude of federal funds needed, Watson also
formed the White House Drought Working Group composed of top
water resources specialists from ten federal agencies. The
"lead agency" role in this working group was given to the
Corps of Engineers. A report, entitled "Drought Appraisal,"
was completed in mid-March after two weeks of intensive interaction.

Based on these several sources of information, the
President's $844 million "drought package" was developed and
transmitted to the Congress through the President's formal
message of March 23.

This proposal to Congress is summarized in Table 1.
Involving seven agencies and nine programs, it represents
the largest single outlay for emergency drought relief in
the nation's history. The first component of the package to
be signed into law (on April 7) was the so-called "Water
Bank Bill" introduced by Senator Henry Jackson in the Senate
and Congressman Lloyd Meeds in the House. Administered by
the Bureau of Reclamation, it is a new authorization providing for the measures briefly described in Table 1. (10)
The second component to take effect involved an apportionment action by the Office of Management and Budget making
available $100 million to the Farmers Home Administration's
Emergency Loan Program for loans to farmers and ranchers for
prospective losses; without the apportionment action, loan
money was available only for actual losses. Five components
of the President's "drought package" involved supplemental
appropriations to existing programs. Four of these--$225
million in loans and grants to small communities for short-
term water supply assistance (Farmers Home Administration),
$100 million in cost sharing grants for soil conservation
measures (Agricultural Conservation Service), $30 million

TABLE 1. THE WHITE HOUSE "DROUGHT PACKAGE"

	AGENCY	PROGRAM DESCRIPTION
Department of Agriculture	Farmers Home Administration (FmHA)	• Emergency Loan Program: $100 million for emergency 5% interest loans to cover prospective losses to farmers and ranchers. • Community Facilities Program: $225 million loan and grant program ($150 million in 5% interest loans; $75 million in grants) for short-term water supply assistance to communities less than 10,000 population.
	Agricultural Stabilization and Conservation Service (ASCS)	• Agricultural Conservation Program: $100 million for soil conservation cost-sharing grants.
	Federal Crop Insurance Corporation (FCIC)	• $50 million to increase FCIC capital stock
Department of the Interior	Bureau of Reclamation	• Drought Emergency Program: The purchase of water to create a water bank for emergency/priority distribution ($75 million), the protection of fish and wildlife ($10 million), grants to states, and 5% loans for water supply and conservation measures. • $30 million for emergency irrigation loans.
	Southwestern Power Administration (SWPA)	• $13.8 million for purchase of emergency power supplies
	Economic Development Administration (EDA), Department of Commerce	• Community Emergency Drought Relief: $225 million loan and grant program ($150 million in 5% interest loans; $75 million in grants) for short-term water supply assistance to communities over 10,000 population.
	Small Business Administration (SBA)	• Community Drought Disaster Program: $50 million for emergency 5% interest loans to small businesses

in an emergency fund for irrigation loans (Bureau of
Reclamation), and $13.8 million to enable the Southwest Power
Administration to purchase electricity from fossil fuel
plants for delivery on power contracts--were signed by the
President on May 4. The other supplemental appropriations
request providing $50 million to increase the capital stock
of the Federal Crop Insurance Corporation (necessary to
allow the FCIC to provide additional crop insurance coverage)
was signed on April 16. Two programs remained: the $225
million loan and grant program to communities over 10,000
population for emergency water supply (a temporary new
authority in the Economic Development Administration), and
the $50 million for low interest Small Business Adminis-
tration loans. The former was signed into law on May 23.
However, while the legislation authorized expenditures at
the $225 million level, the actual amount appropriated was
$175 million. The proposed SBA legislation was tied in
early spring to an omnibus SBA disaster bill and has failed
to pass Congress. [11]

Several weeks after the President submitted the Administration's legislative recommendations to Congress, the
Secretaries of Agriculture, Commerce, and Interior and the
Administrators of the Small Business Administration and the
Federal Disaster Assistance Administration signed a Memorandum of Agreement establishing common procedures for the
designation of Emergency Drought Impact Areas, i.e., for
determining the eligibility of counties for assistance
under the White House "drought package." By April 25, the
date this Memorandum of Agreement was published in the
Federal Register, some 1,200 counties were designated as
eligible for drought emergency relief; by the end of August,
the number had soared to more than 2,200 counties.

The Memorandum of Agreement also established the Federal
Interagency Drought Coordinating Committee composed of
alternates to the signatories to the agreement, with the
alternates to the Secretary of Agriculture and the Administrator of the Federal Disaster Assistance Administration
serving as Chairman and Secretary of the Coordinating
Committee, respectively. Besides the task of determining
the eligibility of counties for emergency relief, the
Coordinating Committee has sought to resolve a variety of
implementation and coordination problems. Indicative of the
work of this committee is the decision to extend the time
limit for completion of projects under the FmHA Community
Facilities Program from November 30, 1977 to April 30, 1978
(to correspond with the required completion date of projects
under the companion program administered by the Economic
Development Administration); and the decision leading to the

transfer of funds (in mid-summer) from the Bureau of
Reclamation's Drought Emergency Program to FmHA's Emergency
Loan Program.

The federal expenditure for drought relief is much
larger than the $800 million resulting from the President's
initiative. The Directory of Federal Drought Assistance
identifies more than forty federal programs which offer
drought assistance in one form or another. Included in
this list are the programs requiring a Presidential,
Secretarial, and/or Agency Administrator's "disaster declaration"--for example the Emergency Feed Grain, Cattle Transportation, and Forest Fire Suppression Programs in the Federal
Disaster Assistance Administration; the Economic Injury and
Physical Disaster Loan Programs in the Small Business
Administration; and the Disaster Payments Program in the
Agricultural Stabilization and Conservation Service. (12)
Included also are numerous on-going programs--for example,
the Emergency Livestock, Farm Operating, Farm Ownership, Soil
and Water, and Irrigation and Drainage Loans Programs in the
Farmers Home Administration; the Emergency Conservation
Measures Program in the Agricultural Conservation and
Stabilization Service; the Economic Adjustment and Public
Works Impact Programs in the Economic Development Administra-
tion (Department of Commerce); and the Unemployment Insurance
Grants, Farm Workers, and CETA Programs in the Employment
and Training Administration (Department of Labor).

Although there are no reliable estimates of how much
federal money has been spent overall in the 1977 drought--
Government Accounting Office has taken no definite steps to
arrive at such an accounting--the total would surely run in
the several billions. The Farmers Home Administration alone
reports that it has spent more than $700 million on some
24,000 drought-related loans exclusive of the two emergency
programs it is administering as part of the White House
"drought package."

By Mid-spring, more than 50 drought-related bills had
been introduced in Congress. Although many of these were
never reported out of, or even referred to, committee, the
sheer number of these bills reflects the prominent position
of the drought problem on the national agenda during the
early months of 1977. Nearly a dozen of the bills called
for changes in legislation related to the Federal Disaster
Assistance Administration. One such bill proposing the
transfer of authority for the Emergency Feed Grain Program
from FDAA to the Department of Agriculture was attached to
the pending Omnibus Farm Bill and was expected to pass.

The federal response to the 1977 drought has involved the creation of new short-term emergency programs by the Administration; swift and supportive action by the Congress; the mobilization and coordination of numerous programs in numerous agencies; the expenditure of large sums of money; and generally good relations with the states, local governments, and private interests. Although numerous "field level" breakdowns in the administration of federal programs could be cited, and red tape and unyielding enforcement of certain rules and regulations have sometimes run counter to administrative intent, the overall federal performance has been decisive and relatively effective in providing timely relief for those in need.

Lingering Problems and Unanswered Questions

Droughts are "creeping phenomena." It is difficult to tell when they begin, how long they will last, and how serious they will be. There can be no doubt that much of the nation has been and continues to be in the grip of a serious drought at this writing. What is less clear is whether the drought will continue, and, if so, what will be its extent, magnitude, and impacts. The basic uncertainty here is that of knowing whether or not precipitation patterns will return to normal (or above).

Notwithstanding this climatic uncertainty--state-of-the-art statistical studies and atmospheric prediction models appear to be unable to resolve the issue--important decisions have to be made in the near future by farmers, state and federal officials, and others. Farmers need to make planting and investment decisions. State officials need to decide whether to continue or to institute new measures designed to mitigate potential drought damages. And, similarly, federal officials need to decide whether additional legislation is needed to reauthorize the emergency assistance programs most of whose funds carry an obligation deadline of September 30, 1977, or to create new programs or revamp old ones to replace these short-term programs.

These decisions are confounded by another kind of uncertainty--uncertainty about the impacts of drought. The case is strikingly portrayed by the fact that record or near-record crops were produced during the 1977 growing season in areas showing low Palmer index values. What does this mean? On the one hand, it means that the drought prevention measures after the droughts of the Thirties and Fifties (especially the soil conservation measures) have made a positive difference, that extensive groundwater pumping for

irrigation has saved crops in many areas, and that the in-
frequent rains have come at just the right times in other
areas. It does not necessarily mean that severe impacts
have permanently been avoided, that soil moisture and groundwater reserves have been replenished, or that lag or side
effects may not occur in the future.

The Palmer index is an aggregate measure of wetness/
dryness computed from the values of a number of parameters
including precipitation, soil moisture, runoff, evaporation,
and groundwater reserve. Being an aggregate measure of
longer-term drought conditions, it is less sensitive to
changes in precipitation than other, single drought indica-
tors (e.g., soil moisture). The upshot of this is that widespread and serious impacts may yet occur, especially if
precipitation continues to be low.

No concrete decisions have (as of mid-September, 1977)
been made on the need or merits of introducing new legislation to reauthorize on a limited time basis the President's
emergency drought programs, or to request additional appropriations for established and on-going drought-related programs, or to assume that the drought will moderate to the
extent that no additional legislation will be required. No
decision has been reached either on whether or not to maintain the Federal Interagency Drought Coordinating Committee.
Meanwhile, the Western Regional Drought Action Task Force
and other state and interstate groups are actively engaged
in the task of assessing potential drought problems, and
can be expected to press for responsive federal (as well as
state) actions if and when the need is perceived. Meanwhile,
too, all parties are waiting for nature to resolve some of
the uncertainty.

Conclusion

Besides the large size of the assistance outlay, several
features of the federal response to the 1977 drought seem
particularly noteworthy. First, the creation of a number
of new, short-term emergency programs constituted a
significant departure from "regular" national disaster
management policy; rather than relying exclusively or even
primarily on established programs, a number of temporary and,
in some instances, almost experimental programs were enacted
--programs which were highly specific to drought problems
(e.g., loans for prospective losses, funds to create a
federal water bank). Second, the states played a significant
role in shaping the character of the federal response.
Existing multistate organizations enabled the states to

aggregate political power and to effectively champion states'
interests in the formulation of the federal response. Third,
the appointment of Jack Watson, the President's Assistant
for Intergovernmental Relations, as the Federal Drought
Coordinator indicates that the drought was perceived initially as largely as intergovernmental relations or
"political" problem. The more recent assignment of staff
from the Domestic Council to deal with lingering issues
(e.g., whether or not new legislation is required to extend
the emergency drought programs and/or provide additional
funds for existing programs; whether or not to retain the
Federal Interagency Drought Coordinating Committee) suggests
that the drought has subsequently come to be viewed from the
federal perspective as more a domestic management problem.

Basic uncertainties about the climatic future, about
impacts yet to come, about the outcome of White House and
Congressional proposals to reorganize and reform the whole
federal disaster establishment, [12] and about the politics
of intergovernmental relations make it nearly impossible to
speculate on the nature and extent of the federal role in
drought mitigation in the months ahead. A sequel to the
federal and states response to the 1977 drought needs to be
written in perhaps another year.

[1]The States participating in the Western Regional Drought
Action Task Force are: California, Oregon, Washington,
Hawaii, Idaho, Montana, Utah, Nevada, Arizona, New
Mexico, Colorado, Wyoming, South Dakota, North Dakota,
Kansas, Nebraska, Illinois, Iowa, Minnesota, Oklahoma
and Texas.

[2]Information for this section was provided by Alex
Cunningham, Deputy Director of California's Drought
Emergency Task Force, in a report entitled "California
Drought Update: July 15, 1977."

[3]Many cities and communities throughout California have
instituted either mandatory or voluntary water rationing programs. Throughout the San Francisco Bay Area,
water use is 30 percent less in 1977 than in 1976 and
some areas have reduced consumption up to 65 percent.
Residential use in some cases has been as low as 25-30
gallons per person per day (about one-sixth of normal).
Many small communities have been out of water and
supplies were hauled by tank truck. Some rural domestic
wells were "de-watered" as groundwater levels fell or
large new, nearby wells were operated.

[4]As reported in the Wells Fargo July "Business Review,"
John Mortimer noted that drought related agricultural
losses in California will probably range from $500
million to $700 million in 1977. Estimated losses in
1976 were $510 million, of which $467 million was
suffered in the livestock industry. Losses in other
sectors of the State's agricultural economy were
expected to increase in 1977, although shifts in crop
patterns and intensive groundwater pumping will help
minimize these losses.

[5]Typically, California derives 28 percent (46.6 billion
kilowatt hours) of its electrical energy from hydro
sources; in 1977 hydro was expected to provide nine
percent (15.5 million kilowatt hours) of the State's
total requirements. This shortfall was expected to
mean the burning of another 50 million barrels of oil
to meet the anticipated electric loads. The cost of
this oil was expected to exceed $700 million.

[6]Information for this section was provided by Jason King,
Chairman of the Ad Hoc Executive Water Emergency
Committee, in a report entitled "Washington Drought
Situation Report: July 12, 1977."

[7]The information contained in this section was obtained
from various state agency reports as provided to the
Western Regional Drought Action Task Force by Lt. Governor
Harvey Wollman.

[8]Quoted from a report entitled "South Dakota Drought
Recovery" available from the office of the Lt.
Governor.

[9]As reported in the September 13, 1976 Weekly Weather and
Crop Bulletin (Vol. 64, No. 37).

[10]As noted earlier, the President signed a bill (S. 1935)
on August 17 which allowed the transfer of the remaining
portion (approximately $70 million) from the "water bank"
program to other programs previously authorized by
S. 925. These funds had to be obligated by September 30,
1977.

[11]Since this proposed legislation was not passed and the
demand for SBA loans from drought-impacted parties (e.g.,
ski area operators) has been great, SBA has made a large
number of loans for actual losses, including loans to
farmers (a new precedent), under its existing disaster
loans programs.

[12]The "emergency drought impact area" designation conferred
by the Federal Interagency Drought Coordinating Committee
(and applicable only to the programs contained in the
White House "drought package") is not a "disaster area"
declaration. Some instances of frustration and difficulty have stemmed from the (mistaken) belief that
designation as an emergency drought area automatically
qualified a county for disaster funds.

9

Forecasting Future Droughts: Is It Possible?

Stephen H. Schneider

Actuarial Forecasts

Considerable recent attention has been focused on American droughts, since (1) the U.S. plains have experienced widespread drought conditions since early 1974, (2) grain produced in the U.S. constitutes a large fraction of available food in the world export market, and (3) some scientists have forecast expanded drought conditions throughout the last of the 1970s, perhaps even as a consequence of pollution. This paper will examine the question: can droughts be forecast?

Before proceeding to forecastability issues, it is clear that droughts have been a repeated feature of our climate. It is well known that in the U.S. plains and western states droughts of some significance have occurred, lasting for periods of roughly three to ten years; and over the past 160 years these droughts have been, roughly speaking, spaced some twenty to twenty-two years apart. Also, they have occurred near alternate minima of the double sunspot cycle. Since the last drought period ended in the mid 1950s and the sun has once again passed through a minima in the 22-year cycle, forecasts have proliferated suggesting that we would, once again, enter a drought period.

However, there are several problems with this "forecast:" (1) no physical theory explaining the alleged connection between the double sunspot cycle and high plains droughts enjoys widespread acceptance, (2) the western U.S. seems to be a somewhat unique place on earth in exhibiting such seemingly cyclic behavior, and (3) the droughts are not precisely aligned with the double sunspot cycle, nor are they geographically comparable, nor do they last for the same time, nor do they exhibit the same severity. Thus, it is not yet clear whether there is a sunspot-drought connection, although

one fact is perfectly clear: droughts of considerable
severity and longevity are precedented and the period between
about 1956 and 1973 enjoyed abnormally good growing conditions in the U.S. plains. Thus, prudence should have suggested preparations for a recurrence of these precedented events,
even if politics had not intervened to the contrary (see
Chapter 4 of The Genesis Strategy: Climate and Global Survival, by S. H. Schneider with L. E. Mesirow (1), for a detailed account of the futile warnings issued by several
scientists to prepare for the inevitability of drought).

But beyond such "actuarial forecasts" which dictate
rough probabilities for future droughts based solely on past
(and often inadequate) statistics, what are the prospects for
forecasting future droughts more specifically? Since drought
is a feature of climate, we must first define what we mean by
climate and then discuss its predictability. And, we must
also recognize that past statistics alone may be an insufficient guide to the future, since not only are the natural
forces that shaped past climates still active, but many
believe human activities could well be competing with nature
as a growing influence on climate (see Chapter 6 of The
Genesis Strategy (1)).

Climatic Definitions

Climate is conventionally defined in terms of suitable
statistics (e.g., means, variances, correlations or frequen-
cies) of a set of weather characteristics such as instantaneous temperature, rainfall, snowfall, cloudiness or wind
speed and direction. The climatic system consists of the
interactive elements of the earth, further divided into the
atmosphere (air), the hydrosphere (water), and the cryosphere
(ice and snow), lithosphere (earth's crust) and the biosphere
(life), of which any may change over the specific (climatic)
time scale of interest. In climatic modeling the "internal
climatic system," those physical processes within the climatic system considered to be interactive, should be further
distinguished from the "external climatic system," or those
boundary conditions outside the climatic system (such as
solar energy input variations) which provide the forcing
functions for the internal system.

The importance of statistical sampling issues in the
investigation of climate should further be recognized in the
consideration of the following definitions (see ref. (2) for
details). A "climatic time series" is defined as the observed sequence of states (e.g., the "weather") of the climatic system, with the "climate" simply being the statistical
properties of the climatic time series. These statistics

are obtained by performing calculations over a time period
referred to as a "climatic sample." The length of the
climatic sample, of course, can be arbitrarily chosen as long
as this period of time is greater than the "weather predictability period" of the atmosphere (i.e., approximately a
month as seen from data and some theoretical considerations).
Indeed, since all finite climatic samples contain an unpredictable fluctuating component known as "climatic noise"
(i.e., the instantaneous state of the atmosphere called
weather), sample statistics will, in general, yield different
results, even if they had common infinite-time statistics.
This difference between the climates of different samples is
what one designates as "climatic change." Since the finite
samples contain unpredictable weather fluctuations, it is
also necessary to define "climatic sampling errors" as the
purely statistical discrepancies between the estimates of the
climatic properties made from the finite samples and the
actual values that would be obtained from an infinite time
sample. For example, one might wish to compare the estimated
mean precipitation for a finite sample for, say, the U.S.
high plains region, with the mean precipitation determined
from an infinite (or at least very long time) sample. However, in practice this infinite time sample (or infinite
record) would just not be available. Thus, through another
approach a comparison of the statistics of the finite sample
can be made with the statistics of what one defines as a
"climatic ensemble," determined from model calculations.
Here, through the introduction of "random" perturbations in
climatic model time simulation experiments (using the identi-
cal boundary conditions and with the number of simulations
generally limited by the constraints imposed by the com-
puter), one generates ensemble statistics which are <u>assumed</u>
to have the statistical properties associated with an infinite stationary time series. Formally, stationary means that
the joint probability distribution of the climatic variables
is independent of the choice of the climatic sampling period,
or more simply, the statistical properties such as means,
variances, covariances, etc. are constant in time.

Consider the above definitions now applied to the
example of the plains with the single chosen climatic
variable--precipitation. On the one hand a comparison of the
statistics of mean precipitation for a set of sequential finite climatic samples may suggest that climatic change is occurring. But, on the other hand, if these finite samples are
compared with a climatic ensemble determined from an appropriate climate model, or perhaps from a very much longer time
period sample if it were available (assumed to be represen-
tative of infinite time statistics), one might conclude that
some fraction of the differences in the mean precipitation

of the sequence of samples is due to climatic noise rather
than a change in equilibrium climate. Thus a major problem
still remains in the data analysis of actual observations or
modeling experiments: to separate a climatic signal (e.g.,
produced by a changed boundary condition) from climatic
noise. This problem is the chief obstacle to forecasting
seasonal anomalies in weather (such as drought), since the
noise is large over such time scales (3).

Some Related Scientific Issues
of Specific Climatic Forecasts:
Predictability, Latency and Detectability

Although natural climatic variability can be expected to
continue with a high degree of certainty and a low degree of
specific predictability (i.e., predictability not based upon
historical probabilities), it still may be possible for
climatologists to provide useful input in the planning process. For example, an actuarial accounting of the likelihood
of climatic fluctuations of natural origin, as pointed out in
the previous section, can be attempted by statistical analyses
of past records. Furthermore, use of mathematical models of
climate can provide estimates of the order-of-magnitude response of the climatic system to pollutants such as carbon
dioxide.

But two issues, latency and detectability, need to be
clarified before estimates of potential pollution effects on
climate can be very useful. These issues are associated with
the identification of a climatic "signal" from, say, a pollu-
tant, in the face of climatic "noise" (e.g., inherent weather
variability--which is unpredictable after several weeks).
This then leads to the broader issues of climatic predictability (i.e., can future climates in fact be predicted?)

Prediction of the climate may be subdivided into two
definitions (4). "Climate predictability of the first kind"
is concerned with predicting "climate" in a sequence. This
differs from predicting a change in the long-term averaged
climate in response to a change in some boundary condition
(such as increased carbon dioxide in the atmosphere, or a
major fluctuation in the solar insolation). This latter
situation is called "climate predictability of the second
kind." An example of the former might be the ability to
foresee the seasonal rainfall for several consecutive seasons
in the future. An example of the latter might be a prediction of global warming from the "greenhouse effect"* of

*"Greenhouse effect" is not strictly appropriate as analogy,
 and thus the term is used loosely for historical continuity.

carbon dioxide if the concentration of atmospheric carbon
dioxide were doubled. The prediction of the second kind
relates nothing about the sequence of climates during the
change to a new long-term climatic state.

Considerable uncertainty exists as to the extent of predictability of either the first or second kind. Some pre-
liminary evidence (5) does suggest that much of the interannual climatic variability of sea-level pressure for a
period of about 70 years can be attributed to unpredictable
fluctuations (i.e., the weather) in the midlatitude regions.
However, there remains some optimism from this pioneering
analysis for considerable skill in regional climatic prediction of the first kind in the tropical and polar regions.
Further work along this line is proceeding with the study of
other climatic variables, although it is certainly hampered
by the lack of a sufficient number of long continuous data
records. This is, of course, not the last word in predictability studies, but it is true that whether prediction of
the first kind is even possible is still unknown.

Some dramatic empirical evidence does exist, however,
for predictability of the second kind associated with major
external forcings. That is, a reasonably predictable climatic response occurs each year: the seasonal cycle. Thus, we
can expect that as models of the climatic system improve in
their capability to reproduce a seasonal cycle, they then
will be more able to simulate the sensitivity of the climatic
system to other large external forcings. The magnitude of an
anthropogenic (or other external) perturbation to a boundary
condition of the system might also be expected to govern the
magnitude of the climatic response. Unfortunately, scientists face another problem since not all variations in
boundary conditions or other external conditions are themselves predictable (for example, no one can say presently
when the next geophysical event, such as a volcanic eruption
that spews dust into the atmosphere, will occur). Uncertainty in other boundary conditions along with "climatic noise"
caused by unpredictable weather fluctuations can often mask
any correlation between the response of the climatic system
and a variation in a particular boundary condition that might
be under study.

It is also important to note that because of the problem
of identifying climatic signals, certain climatic changes may
occur and may even be predictable, although not for an
extremely long lag time. This problem, referred to earlier
as "latency," may arise for two reasons. First, geophysical
processes have certain inherent time constants associated
with them, which may be as short as a fraction of a second

(e.g., molecular relaxation times) or as long as millenia
(e.g., glacial size changes). For instance, chlorofluoromethanes released near the earth's surface as aerosol spray
propellants may take years to gradually diffuse to the
stratosphere, where these chlorofluoromethanes will be de-
graded through the process of photolysis, thereby producing
chlorine atoms believed to be involved in ozone gas destruction. This delay in the actual climatic effect (relative to
the time of effluence) is governed by the time scales of
atmospheric transport and chemistry; thus the ozone destruction may be delayed for decades after the initial release of
the chlorofluoromethanes. Similarly, a glacial advance or
retreat, might be delayed long after a global cooling or
warming event.

A second problem for the scientist wishing to establish
the sensitivity of the climatic system to an external perturbation relates to the time delay involved in establishing the
detectability of the perturbation. Because of the inherent
variability, an important signal of climatic change may not
be evident for a long time because of the noise in the climatic system--again implying a latent period before which the
signal strength relative to the noise is sufficiently large
as to be judged "detectable." For a constant-strength signal, statistical techniques (including ordinary time-averaging)
do exist for increasing the signal-to-noise ratio, but sufficient data from observations or model experiments are still
required. A case in which the signal-to-noise ratio would be
expected to increase say, a global temperature increase from
carbon dioxide which is monotonically accumulating in the
atmosphere from fossil fuel combustion (if, in actuality this
dominates other potential anthropogenic or nonanthropogenic
changes)(6). Even if this is the case, the ratio may not be
judged statistically significant until the effect has reached
what may be called a "threshold of detectability." (Perhaps
"threshold" is too vague a term here and the appropriate
concept should be expressed as a probabilistic confidence
limit.) It is this "threshold of detectability," which
occurs at some chosen value of signal-to-noise ratio, above
which the possibility of climatic change is highly probable.
The magnitude of the threshold would certainly depend on such
factors as the climatic time period under study, the inherent
variability of the climatic system, and the accuracy and
spatial coverage of the instrumental observations of climatic
variables. One may compare this type of threshold to an
"effects threshold" (a concept often used in toxicology),
below which no effect is present as a result of the particular agent of insult. An effects threshold may exist for some
anthropogenic insults or changed boundary conditions that
perturb the climatic system sufficiently to excite some

atmospheric or climatic instability (such as cloud formation).
However, it is more likely that any large-scale climatic
changes caused by a continuously varying boundary condition
or a continuously increasing insult (e.g., an anthropogenic
emission) will be characterized by a continuously increasing
climatic change (with perhaps some latency delay). Thus, the
concept of a threshold of detectability becomes more useful
for the purposes of determining a climatic change than the
more classical concept of an effects threshold.

In view of these issues of latency and detectability, it
is problematical that the tentative estimates of state-of-the-
art models often cannot be verified from actual data until a
large, perhaps irreversible, climatic change has already occurred. Does this mean that we should hedge against not only
the uncertainties of natural climatic variability, but also
those of anthropogenic climatic changes that present models
may be able to predict? Existing models do enable predictions
of the second kind to be made of major climatic effects, although presently they cannot incorporate all the potentially
important physical and chemical interactions.

Summary and Conclusions

It is apparent from previous sections, that little
drought forecast skill now exists, and that even the prospects for improved skill are hard to assess. Furthermore, we
do know that droughts are a repeated feature of such different climatic regions as the Asian monsoon lands and the
midlatitude great plains. Yet, these regions have the climates they do because of vastly different features of the
global atmospheric circulation, which is itself a consequence
of the land/sea distribution and the differential heating of
the earth. Thus, it is not obvious that causes of drought in
monsoon-dependent India would be related to those of the central U.S. But, even though it is a cliché to say that "everything in the climatic system is connected to everything
else," it is thus, not unlikely that unusual features or
systematic changes in one large climatic region of the earth
will be coupled to changes in many other places. Since the
circulation patterns are forced by differential heating of
the earth, legitimate concern has been expressed over such
questions as CO_2-induced warming of the earth or changes in
the brightness or water carrying capacity of land surface
from deforestation, agriculture and overgrazing (7). These
human activities perturb natural energy flows and thus they
can change accustomed circulation features such as monsoon
belts, or midlatitude granaries--so located by the position
of the jet stream winds. Although such changes would seem
negligible to those still within the influence of their

accustomed climatic features, those at the margin of dis-
placed circulation features could experience radical departures from their climatic expectations if circulation patterns
shifted with slowly varying climatic trends--whether of
natural or of human origin.

Given these possibilities, the drought in the northern
U.S. plains and western states that plagued the region
throughout much of the 1974 to 1977 period has been "explained" by many theories. These range from long-term climatic trends to anomalies in Pacific Ocean surface temperatures, to sunspots, to stratospheric warming in polar regions,
to air pollution and even to agriculture in the U.S. midwest.
Presently, the real cause (or combination of causes) remains
speculative, although the consequence on water supply, soil
erosion and grain yields is more easily documented.

In conclusion, then, society may need to plan for climatic events like droughts that can now be deemed only probable.
In some cases, scientifically specified confidence limits can
be obtained, although in others the range of uncertainty sur-
rounding present estimates cannot even be quantified-and the
best that can be done is to assess the intuition of the
experts. Hope still remains, however, for a narrowing of
these uncertainties. Meanwhile, a difficult question to consider is how long society should wait for more certain knowledge of drought predictability before undertaking the implementation of hedging policies to mitigate its consequences.

References

(1)   S. H. Schneider with L. E. Mesirow, The Genesis Strategy,
       Climate and Global Survival (Plenum, New York, 1976; and
       Delta, New York, 1977), 419 pp.

(2)   C. E. Leith, GARP Publication Series 16, WMO, Geneva,
       Switzerland, 137-142 (1975).

(3)   R. M. Chervin, W. M. Washington and S. H. Schneider, J.
       Atmos. Sci., 33, 413-423 (1976).

(4)   E. N. Lorenz, GARP Publication Series 16, WMO, Geneva,
       Switzerland, 132-137 (1975).

(5)   R. A. Madden, Mon. Wea. Rev., 104, 942-952 (1976).

(6)   S. H. Schneider and R. D. Dennett, Ambio, 4, 65-74 (1975).

(7)   J. Otterman, Climatic Change, 1, No. 2 (1977, in press).

(8)   The National Center for Atmospheric Research is sponsored
       by the National Science Foundation.

Index